Marriage:
Two Hearts,
One Heartbeat

Omawumi Efueye

authorHOUSE®

AuthorHouse™ UK
1663 Liberty Drive
Bloomington, IN 47403 USA
www.authorhouse.co.uk
Phone: 0800.197.4150

Published by AuthorHouse 12/17/2015

ISBN: 978-1-5049-4651-3 (sc)
ISBN: 978-1-5049-9562-7 (e)

Print information available on the last page.

DEDICATION

This book is dedicated to Pastors Gbolahan Faluade and Babs Balepo.

G. Falu, though we were childhood friends, you gave your life to Christ about ten years before I did and became an inspiration, an encourager, and indeed a mentor to me. You introduced me to the vital family/ministry balance and thus ultimately saved my marriage.

Pastor Babs, God sent you to mediate in our marriage when it had absolutely hit rock-bottom. Your godly counsel and wisdom set us on the path of recovery, revitalisation and becoming a restorative reference point.

For every relationship enhanced and sanctified, for every marriage conducted, saved and strengthened by this book you will doubtless be partakers in the rewards.

Thank you and may God continue to bless your own marriages and homes.

Acknowledgement

I would like to start by thanking our Heavenly Father, Abba, the Author and Perfecter of the institution of marriage and the One "from whom every family in heaven and on earth is named." (Ephesians 3:15 BBE). It is a measure of His mercy, love and awe-inspiring grace that He has chosen someone as eminently unqualified in pedigree, experience and scholarship as I am, to write on a subject as critical as marriage is to societal well-being.

I also want to thank my darling wife who has endured me, warts and all, for three decades (and still counting!) It is because you did not give up on me that I have a relevant story to tell. My children, natural and spiritual could not ask for a better mother. I will never stop declaring that you remain the best investment I ever made.

My two children, Dede and Marcel deserve kudos for weathering all the storms that come with being "PK's" (Pastor's Kids). In spite of all the pressures and unrealistic expectations people have placed on you, you have been swayed but not broken by the winds of affliction. Remain strong in the Lord and in the power of His might.

A big shout out to everyone who has been involved in the former Forever Friends and now Friends4Life classes: Bebe Ojukwu, Ronke Faboro, Ngozi Aligwekwe, Rovi Oluwole, Mabinty Esho, Christina Constantinou, and many others. You had all been begging me on to write a text for the course and classes. Now you can see the birth of the dream.

Bebe and Mabinty, thank you for typing and editing and putting the Text and Workbook together. Obi Ejiogu (Obi 1), thank you for the dispatch with which you produced the very vivid and apt illustrations for the Workbook.

The core community of Chapel of Life deserve particular mention. Victor and Biola Odunlami, Uche and Ify Oti, Demola Soremekun, Sumbo and Niyi Aderinola, Sade Abiodun, Dapo Akinola, Demola Grillo, Patrick and Nadia Egbuchiem and the rest of the COL family. In such a short time you have established, according to God's desire and pattern, "a church without walls". In this environment I believe godly relationships will evolve and thrive and marriages that glorify God will blossom. Thank you for believing in and supporting me and the God-breathed vision.

To Bidemi and Bukky Arowolo I want to say words cannot express the depth of love and gratitude that suffuses my heart when I think of your love, sacrifice and unrelenting support for me and all my projects. God who sees in private will surely reward you openly.

I cannot but acknowledge Jide and Bukky George who for my ordination in August 1997 gave me, as a present, the life-changing book "Marriage as God Intended" by Selwyn Hughes. The copious references made from that book in this one is a testament to Rev.(Dr) Selwyn Hughes as one of the foremost marriage counsellors in his generation. It also eloquently testifies to the wisdom, insight and practicality that characterised his life and ministry. He remains one of my mentors even though I never had the privilege of a face-to-face meeting but I'm encouraged by the thought that he is enjoying 'Everyday With Jesus'!

Foreword

Over the years I have been asked to write commendations for a number of marriage courses. This is not always easy as those of us who preach are bound to have different ways of presenting the many sensitive issues that such courses involve. Furthermore, alongside abiding truths there will always be cultural considerations that have to be taken into account. Here, though, is a course that comes from a man who is not only well-versed in Scripture but is also capable of empathising appropriately with his audience. Pastor Efueye has taught this course many times and I am delighted that he is now making it available for a wider public.

Here you will find wisdom on every page, coupled with scrupulous honesty. Each chapter is full of biblical truth set in a culturally relevant context. Pastor Efueye is a man who is prepared to share his heart freely to ensure that marriages are built on the best possible foundation. I think no-one can ask more of a marriage course than this. No matter what cultural lens you are looking through as you read it, the clarity and openness with which Pastor Efueye writes will be a blessing. His enthusiasm for marriage is bound to inspire you.

Some marriage courses read rather like the workshop manual a garage mechanic might use for fixing a car – endless descriptions of nuts and bolts, with instructions for dis-assembling and re-assembling the parts. This course is no less practical but it is written with a passion for the vehicle as a whole that demands it receives the utmost respect. If you treat your marriage the way this course recommends, it will last a lifetime and give you a safe and rewarding journey through life. Just make sure you share the driving!

Dr Hugh Osgood
Founder and President, Churches in Communities International

WORKBOOK

INTRODUCTION

Overview

- Britain has the highest divorce rate in the European Union (EU) according to a 2014 survey.
- The number of divorces throughout the EU is on the increase, with an average of 1.8 divorces for every 1,000 people.
- In Britain and in Finland the rate is 2.8 divorces per 1,000 marriages, compared with just 0.6 per 1,000 in Luxembourg.
- But while the divorce rate in the West has increased slightly during the 1990s, the rate of births outside marriage has risen sharply: more than one child in four was born outside marriage in the EU in 1999, compared with fewer than one in five in 1989.
- The figures vary widely between EU member states, ranging from just 4% of births outside marriage in Greece to 55% in Sweden. Britain is well above the 26% EU average, at 38.8%.

- Statistics show that 45% of marriages in the UK currently end in divorce;
- Second marriages end in divorce in 75% of cases;
- Third marriages end in divorce in 99% cases;
- In the United States, over 50% of first marriages end in divorce, 67% of second marriages end in divorce, and nearly 74% of third marriages end in divorce.

The Root Causes of Marital Disintegration

Several factors are responsible for the fragile state of the noble institution of marriage today:

1. Firstly, we are all products of our _______________ and _______________.

   ➢ Educating oneself and renewing one's mind, as the Bible eloquently puts it, are the keys to _______________ and _______________ _______________.

2. Secondly, nine out of ten people who get married do not know the ______________ of marriage.

    - ______________ love is not enough to sustain a marriage.
    - Many people marry for the wrong reasons and forget that where ______________ is unknown, ______________ is inevitable.
    - If your primary reason for getting married is ______________ then your relationship will inevitably self-destruct, as it feeds on the fuel of its own insatiable appetites.

3. Third is the issue of premarital sex.

    - People need to know the ______________ of sex, its purpose, boundaries, implications, benefits and the ______________ of its misuse and abuse.
    - Sex is not merely ______________ but it involves and engages the ______________ and ______________ of the participants.
    - When you have sex with someone before you marry them, even when and if you finally do, you will have sown into the foundation of the marriage ______________ and a spirit of ______________, or in modern-speak, ______________.

4. Fourthly, marriage as God intended it has been under ferocious attack from counterfeit ______________ masquerading as viable ______________.

    - From immediately after the ______________, man through his religious traditions and culture began to devise hedonistic alternatives to God's one-man-one-wife injunction.
    - Men love the provision in one religion that you can have up to four wives as long as you can love them all ______________. However, no man in history has ever been able to love two wives equally, let alone four! Jacob, Elkanah and David, to name but three, are eloquent biblical testimonies to this fact.

5. The fifth factor, and by far the most subtle, prevalent and insidious threat to the institution of marriage, is ______________.

    - To cohabit is defined as ______________ ______________, especially as husband and wife, without being married.
    - Cohabitation in Great Britain does not qualify to be the functional ______________ of, or indeed a lasting alternative to, ______________.

- There are many ______________ effects of cohabitation on cohabiting parents and their children, when compared to married couples and their offspring.
- Married couples and their children enjoy on the whole more qualitative ______________ circumstances, superior emotional well-being and better physical and mental health.
- If couples want legal protection and the social benefits of making a commitment they should ______________.

6. The sixth and final factor contributing to the rapidly increasing rate of divorce is inadequate ______________.

   - ______________ is not the best teacher, contrary to what that old adage teaches.
   - Other people's experience is a better teacher. A ______________ person learns from other people's mistakes, while a ______________ learns from his own.
   - Education on issues like conflict resolution, changing negative styles of communication, correcting unrealistic expectations about marriage, recognising socio-cultural differences, dealing constructively with different attitudes about vital issues and learning to handle parents and in-laws would all go a long way to eliminating marital disharmony.

7. Conclusion

Whatever the situation, a good marriage doesn't just fall into your lap! So before you take that vital step of entering into the mysterious world of marriage, take the time to go through the necessary preparations. You'll be glad you did, and the ______________ will not only abound but will also abide.

Answers to Introduction

1. backgrounds, experiences, emancipation, progressive transformation
2. purpose, romantic, purpose, abuse, selfish
3. origins, consequences, physical, souls, spirits, distrust, harlotry, prostitution
4. incarnations, alternatives, Fall, equally
5. cohabitation, living together, equivalent, marriage, negative, economic, marry
6. preparation, experience, wise, fool
7. fruit

Chapter 1

HE WHICH MADE THEM FROM THE BEGINNING...

Chapter Overview

- When God created man, His goal was that man would be a reflection of Himself, a kind of cosmic looking glass through which all of creation would get a glimpse of a multi-faceted Creator.
- When picking a life partner, one of your mottos should be 'Beware of the Beasts'!
- Marriages today must come back to the place where spouses are completely open before each other, and do not place any thing or person above each other and the joint interests of their union.
- The marriages that succeed are those in which the man never stops chasing, never stops wooing, never stops sticking to his wife. The wife, on her part, never gets cynical or ceases to respond to the love-call of her life-mate.
- Few things are as attractive and deeply comforting as a romantic septuagenarian, octogenarian or nonagenarian couple. Their marriage has stood the test of time and they are still standing, and indeed still cleaving.
- Marriage is God's idea.

A) Man, God's Mirror (image)

- First indicator of the reflection: man is a singular entity comprising three different distinct parts: ______, ______ and ______.
- Second indicator: man was created as both ______ and ______.
- Third indicator: Man is a personal being with the inbuilt capacity to ______, to ______ and to ______ ______ in decision-making.
- The triune ______ of man reflects the ______ of God.

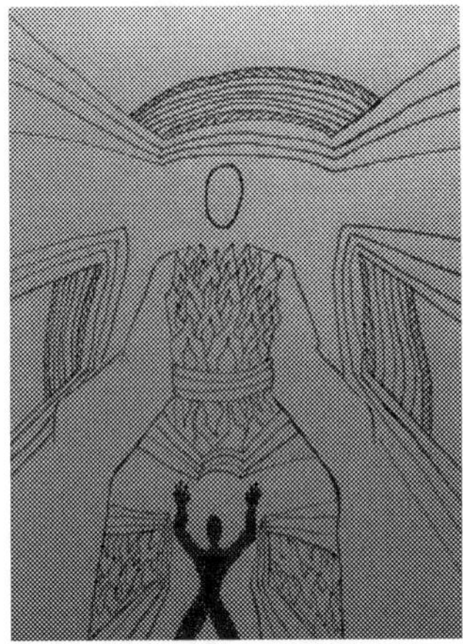

B) Woman, Man's Mirror (image)

- 'Alone' is a compounding of two words: ________ and ________.
- God's solution to Adam being alone was to make Adam a help ________ for him.

The literal Hebrew translation of the phrase 'meet for him' is superbly enlightening as it reads 'as before him'. This carries the obvious connotation of a reflection. So as man is the image and likeness of God, the woman is the image and reflection of man.

C) The Test

- Every time God utters a word or prophecy, that word must be ____________ (Psalm 18:30).
- God establishes His purpose for the as-yet-uncreated woman as Adam's companion and helper.
- God then brought every form of animal and bird to Adam 'to see what he would call them'. This was the first test.
- So having spoken to Adam, God was testing him by bringing the animals to him to see what he would call them.

This exercise was designed by God to achieve at least three objectives:

1. Adam was exercising his God-given ____________.
2. Adam's desire for a partner was awakened by the fact that all the living creatures were in pairs.
3. Adam was invited to search for a companion as he named all existing animals. It was, however, a test which he passed when he found none to be suitable for him.

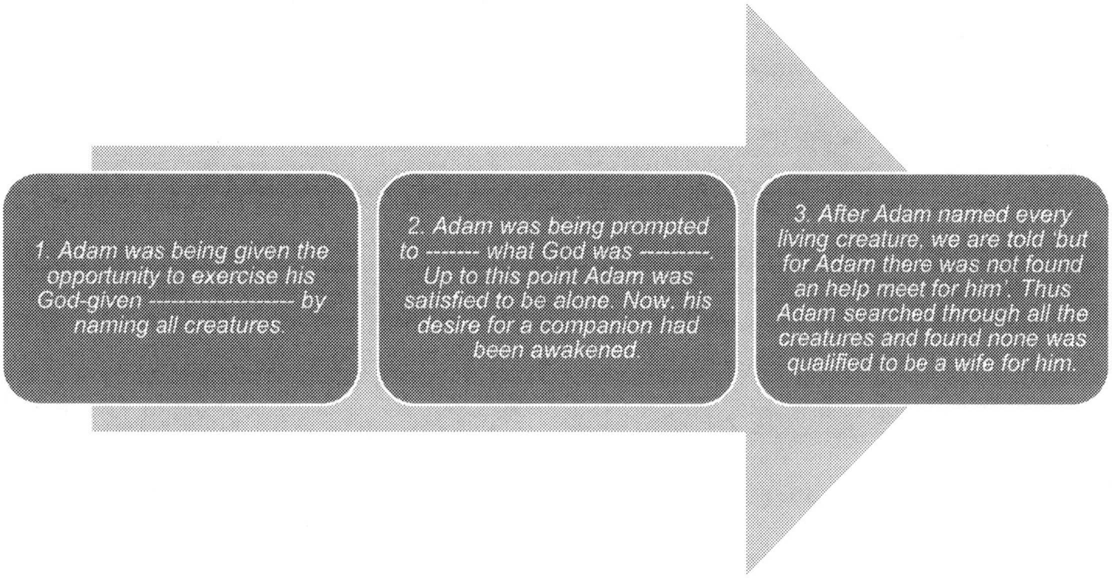

1. Adam was being given the opportunity to exercise his God-given ------------------ by naming all creatures.

2. Adam was being prompted to ------- what God was --------. Up to this point Adam was satisfied to be alone. Now, his desire for a companion had been awakened.

3. After Adam named every living creature, we are told 'but for Adam there was not found an help meet for him'. Thus Adam searched through all the creatures and found none was qualified to be a wife for him.

God was giving Adam the opportunity to search through all the creatures to see if any was qualified to be his life companion.

But an invaluable lesson from Adam's experience is that Adam's search, on his own, yielded no fruit. Unless God builds, one builds in vain and unless He watches over a city, the sentries keep a fruitless vigil.

1. Once Adam had passed this first test, 'the Lord God caused a deep ________ to fall upon Adam, and he ________'.
2. Next, God took one of Adam's ________ and after closing the man's side, the Lord made a ________ out of the rib.

- Man was *created.*
- Woman was formed, moulded, sculpted, pretty much like one would a work of art, a sculptural masterpiece. This explains why women are infinitely more attractive than men. It is a 'design imperative'.

3. In the second and final test, God then brought the woman to Adam (to see what he would call her) and Adam declared: 'So I will name her Woman!' (Genesis 2:23 CEV).
4. Adam knew who he was, and so was able to recognise his ________ in the woman.

D) Key Models of Marriage

1. First key: Therefore a man shall leave his ________ and ________ and be joined to his wife and they shall become ________ ________

2. Second key: Marriage is for men.

   - A man has to be ________ before he can get married.
   - It also takes a man to realise that a more intimate relationship is forged between spouses than can subsist even between parents and their offspring.

3. Third key, of even greater significance: God's statement points to marriage as a universal institution that transcends race, colour, and ethnic or geographical limitations, because God talked of a mother, which was still an unknown concept.

4. Fourth key: There is a progression, a growth, that comes with marriage, and it is signified by the word 'cleave'.

   - To cleave also figuratively means to catch by pursuit.
   - To get a wife in the first place, a man has to ________ and ________ a woman.
   - Many men, once they get and marry their wives, are ignorant of the fact that the real pursuit has only just begun.

5. Fifth key: The man and his wife shall be one flesh. This is obviously referring to the sexual union. Sex has four purposes: a) ________; b) ________; c) ________; and d) ________.

6. Sixth key: Maintaining openness and honesty as a vital rule of marriage was established from the onset. It is written that the man and his wife were together and were both naked, but were unashamed.

The breakdown of family values, and the predominant dysfunctional setting into which most children are born and grow up, means most adults come into the nuptial state with a lot of excess baggage, and many secrets and insecurities.

7. Seventh and more obscure key: This deals with a topical and controversial issue in today's post-modern, permissive and over-liberal society. The phrase 'the man and his wife' refers to the sexes of the partners and their sexuality. God by this statement was establishing His new institution between opposite sexes, leaving no room in His word and counsel for same-sex unions.

E) <u>This is a great mystery...</u>

'Purpose is the reason for which something is done or made.'

1. In his Epistle to the Ephesian Church Paul refers to three important ________ categories:

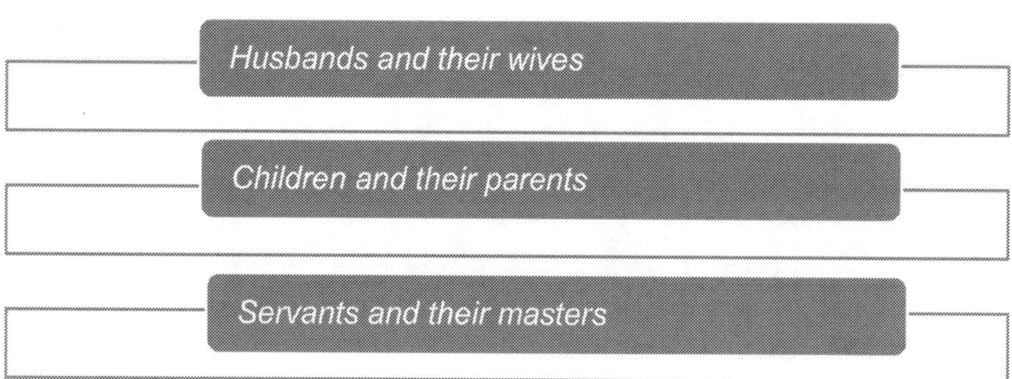

2. Mutual ________ is one of marriage's most potent and effective weapons because it reflects the very nature and character of the Godhead.

3. A ________ heart also knows that the instruction about domination is to dominate creation and creatures and circumstances, and never to dominate one another or other human beings.
4. The wife is to ________ to her own husband as she would to the Lord. This is because:

   - the husband is the head of the wife,
   - just as Christ is the Saviour and Head of the church, which is His own body.

5. As the church is under Christ's ________, wives must likewise be under the rule of their husbands in all things.

And to the husbands...

6. The man is to love his wife as much as Christ loved the ________ and gave His life for it.

   - Men are therefore to love their wives as they love their very own selves;
   - To love your wife is to show that you love yourself;
   - A man and wife have become 'one flesh' (Ephesians 5:31).

7. You thought marriage was about a man and a woman, and about you and your spouse, but rather God had devised the institution to illustrate the otherwise inexplicable relationship between Christ and the Church:

   - The wife does not submit to her husband because he is stronger, wiser, better, richer or superior to her, but because she sees him as representing the amazing love of Christ and His benevolent and loving headship of the Church.
   - She understands that she is reflecting the role of the Church as it yields to Jesus' transformative headship.
   - Likewise, a man does not love his wife sacrificially to the point of laying down his life, as it were, because she has an hourglass figure, 'legs that go on forever', a meek and submissive spirit, or any of the other myriad of reasons for which men marry.
   - Rather, he understands himself to be representative of Jesus' propitiatory love for the Church, sacrificing and providing for, as well as protecting, his wife.

8. While a good deal of romance and sensual attraction are crucial to initiate a marriage and sustain it in the early days, a great deal more is required for a solid foundation and medium- to long-term success. These include: friendship and companionship, loyalty and commitment, fidelity and patience, and – most importantly – unconditional love and acceptance of one's spouse.

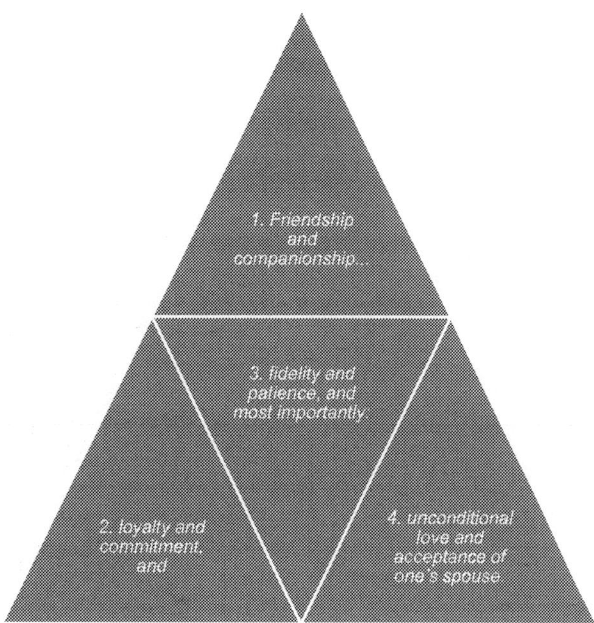

Conclusion

With this understanding of the purpose of marriage, constantly ask yourself: What picture of Christ am I supposed to be portraying? Living with purpose constantly in view is interesting. There are times when you do the right thing, and instantly get the right responses and the right results; and there are times when you feel foolish or are taken for a fool and will see no possible benefit, in the short, medium or long term, to doing what you know to be the right thing.

Finally, and more importantly, however, God intended your marriage to be a beacon to many as they navigate the storm-tossed, iceberg-ridden and shark-infested oceans of the marital expedition.

Application Section

HE WHICH MADE THEM FROM THE BEGINNING…

This Application Section consists of two sections: the individual section and the interactive section. Make sure you have enough time to interact with each other during the interactive section.

Individual (Spouse) Section

Set the scene: Remain together as a couple, but complete this section on your own.

Goal: To gain knowledge about yourself as a reflection of God.

Directions: Get a pen and paper and write your answers to these next questions.

1. State five ways in which you can reflect God's attributes in your marriage.
2. (To the husband) - How do you (or will you), continue (or start) to chase and woo your wife in marriage? Make a firm plan towards this now with dates, times and venues.
3. (To the wife) - How do you (or will you) respond as a wife to your husband's wooing?

Interactive (Couple) Section

Set the scene: Couple to stay together in a private area to talk freely.

Goal: To gain knowledge about each other and your vision and view of the purpose of your marriage.

Directions:

- Discuss your goals, individually and maritally.
- Discuss the purpose of your marriage, as you both now understand it, and how this differs from your initial reasons and purposes for getting married.
- Discuss your understanding of mutual submission, and how this may have affected your marriage negatively or positively. Outline ways in which you will both start to submit to each other.

Homework

1. Read this book together: *Marriage as God Intended*, by Selwyn Hughes.
2. Discuss the following: Any influences in your marriage. Are these positive or negative influences? Have there been any results or issues arising from these influences in your marriage?

Answers to Chapter 1

1. spirit, soul, body
2. male, female
3. rationalise, feel, exercise choices
4. nature, nature
5. all, one
6. meet
7. tried
8. dominion
9. see, seeing
10. sleep, slept
11. ribs, woman
12. reflection
13. father, mother, one flesh
14. mature
15. pursue, woo
16. procreation, recreation, consummation, illustration.
17. relationship
18. submission
19. spirit-led
20. submit
21. authority
22. Church

Chapter 2

ROLES: THEY DETERMINE RELATIONSHIPS, YOU KNOW

Chapter Overview

In marriages, the husband and wife should recognize and agree to their ________ and ________; a clear understanding of well-defined roles will eliminate conflict and confusion.

In a lot of situations, roles determine relationships, and this also applies to marriage.

- In a supermarket, the store employees are responsible for setting items out on the shop floor shelves and maintaining their order. This saves customers from going into the stock room to get items for themselves. The customers are responsible for paying for their purchases before they leave the store. These clear roles help to create and maintain a successful transactional relationship.

Think of three other situations where having clearly defined roles helps to ensure a good working relationship, and prevent confusion.

i. ____

ii. ____

iii. ____

A. THE HUSBAND – A LOVING AND SACRIFICIAL SERVANT LEADER

- God designed marriage to be a partnership of two __________ but the husband is called to be the __________, the head of the union.

 **Ephesians 5v23**

- The husband is the leader in a marriage.
- Husbands are therefore called to exercise loving and sacrificial __________ leadership.
- God thereby designed marriage and its product, family, to be the fundamental and umbilical institution of all societies.

PRACTICAL WAYS FOR A MAN TO LOVE LIKE CHRIST

God so loved the world that He gave His Son to save it. Jesus, in like manner, 'came not to be ministered unto, but to minister, and to give His life as a ransom for many' (Matthew 20:28). A husband is called to do no less in the following areas:

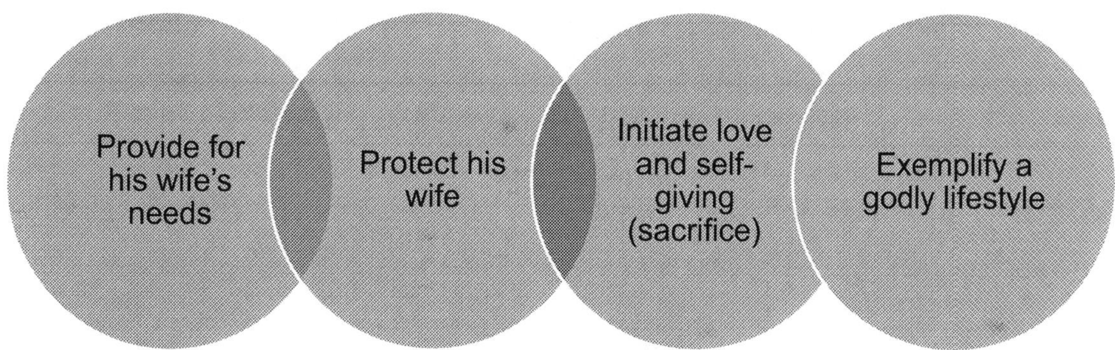

1. Provide for his wife's needs:

   a) A wife's spiritual needs: the husband is to encourage his wife's __________ with God and teach her what he knows of God; the husband is to ensure that his family is an active part of a living, vibrant, Bible-believing Church. The household is also not to forsake __________ with other believers.

1 Corinthians 14:35, Genesis 18:19 and Joshua 24:5

b) A wife's financial needs:

- Financially, the man is to provide for his wife and children by being the primary ______________ of the family.

c) A wife's social needs:

- being __________ to is one of a woman's deepest needs.
- treating wives with ______________ rules out jesting that degrades them personally.

Colossians 3:19 (KJV)

Men are to live with their wives faithfully, tenderly and gently, without grudges or bitterness.

2. Protect his wife:

a) A husband must educate his wife to take ______________ for her choices, actions and reactions.
b) The man must live what he believes and ______________ Christ-like thoughts, motives, words and actions.
c) The husband must also ______________ his wife from herself. When she lets her emotions rule her, she will make some decisions that are contrary to the law of faith.
d) The wife must also be protected from ____________ members, both hers and especially her husband's.
e) A good husband has the responsibility also of protecting his wife from ______________ who would call her attention from the many benefits she enjoys, to the one or two things ___________ from her life and relationships.

Protect Your Treasure. Do not allow strangers and untrustworthy people to gain unlimited access to your assets. If Adam had exercised his God-given dominion and chased the serpent out of his wife's presence and the Garden, neither he nor we would have ended up in the mess we all now find ourselves in.

f) Lastly, a good husband must protect his wife from physical danger.

3. Initiating love and self-giving (sacrifice):

    a) Husbands, your wives also ____________ the habitual tender touch, that is the touch that does not necessarily lead to sex but just establishes contact with her.

4. Exemplifying a godly lifestyle:

    a) The husband must ______________ Christ, who never asked His disciples to do anything that He Himself did not do first.

A. RESPONSIBILITIES OF A GODLY MAN:

____________ the affairs of the family by divine wisdom and with vital input from his wife, holding his wife in ____________, satisfying her ____________ and ensuring her ____________ well-being (spirit, soul and body) are all additional responsibilities a godly man has to perform.

Q. Why does the husband sacrifice for his wife?

CHOOSE ONE OPTION FROM BELOW:

1. Because women are submissive, or to make them so.
2. As a means to an end.
3. Because God has commanded it.

B. RESPONSIBILITY OF WIVES

Women, on their part, do not submit to their husbands because of their sacrificial love or servant-leadership, but in __________ to God's word and will.

1 Peter 3:5–6 regarding Sarah: 'It is said of them ... being in subjection to their own husbands: even as Sarah obeyed Abraham, calling him lord: whose daughters ye are...'

1. Firstly: a wife is to __________ and __________ her husband. Another word for 'help' is 'assist'. This means the husband has a vision or task and still has the lead in taking action, but the wife plays a vital role in helping him fulfil it.

Food for thought: Can you help if there is nothing to help with? Women, you must marry a man with a goal, a vision: not just any goal/vision but a good one, given to him by God.

A woman must contribute to __________ processes in the home.

Most decisions will be agreed upon in consultation, so a good wife must not be reluctant or timid, but graciously air her views.

2. Secondly: a wife must __________ to her husband.

3. Thirdly: a wife is to __________ and __________ her husband. The very purpose of a woman's creation was to help her husband.

Since respect must be earned and begets itself, what does a woman do when her husband is irresponsible, childish and disrespectful to his wife?

God's instruction to marital partners is not to respect your spouse, but to treat them with respect; so a wife must 'treat her husband with respect even if she is unable to respect him as a person, or respect his judgement'.

4. Fourthly: she must share sexual __________ with her husband.

- God in His infinite wisdom is the author of sex and He introduced it as a vital part of marriage when He declared that a man would not only leave his parents and cleave to his wife, but also become 'one flesh' with her. Without sex a couple simply ________ as co-tenants, not husband and wife. Did you know that if a couple marry legally and do not consummate their marriage through the sexual union, the marriage is considered null and void without even the need to go to a divorce court?

- Husband and wife are not to deprive each other of sex, except by mutual consent for a season of fasting and prayer. This is, however, not to be taken to extremes.
- A woman is to meditate sexually on her husband like the Shunammite bride in Songs of Solomon.

 Songs of Solomon 5:10–16; 7:10.

However, even when you and your spouse are not having sex, for some reason or another, and even in trying circumstances, **God still expects self-control and purity**.

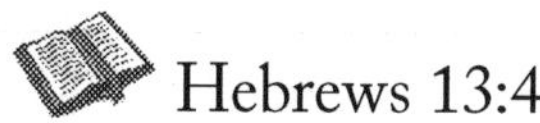 Hebrews 13:4.

1. Fifthly: a wife is responsible for ________ of the household.

- Once the children are born, their daily care, the preparation of meals for the family and keeping the house clean and in order, all fall to the female sex **but** the management of the children and the home is not solely for the wife to execute. Men must be as much a part of their children's growth, development and upbringing as women are, and must carry out some of the tasks of the home. Who carries out what tasks must be agreed between husband and wife.
- After all, though the woman is called to be the manager of the home, the husband still has the **obligation** of managing his wife.

C. FIGHTING AGAINST UNMET ________

- Unmet expectations are responsible for the biggest and most conflicts in marriages.
- Traditionally, one of the greatest areas of ________ relates to children.
- 'Division of labour' is a term in economics that speaks formally of the need to define and split household chores and responsibilities.

Here are some vital steps to take, to ensure that your marriage does not fall into the trap of insurmountable conflicts born of unmet expectations:

- Make a comprehensive list of chores and responsibilities, not leaving out even those things that you know are controversial for your spouse.
- Discuss extensively why you feel strongly about certain roles, so that you can decide with your spouse how to share these roles between you.

A typical list of expectations should thus evolve:

For husbands:

- Responsible for main income
- Pay mortgage/rent, school fees, insurance etc
- Gardening, dustbins, DIY, home maintenance
- Drop children off at school in the morning
- Put kids to bed at night and take them to weekend extracurricular activities

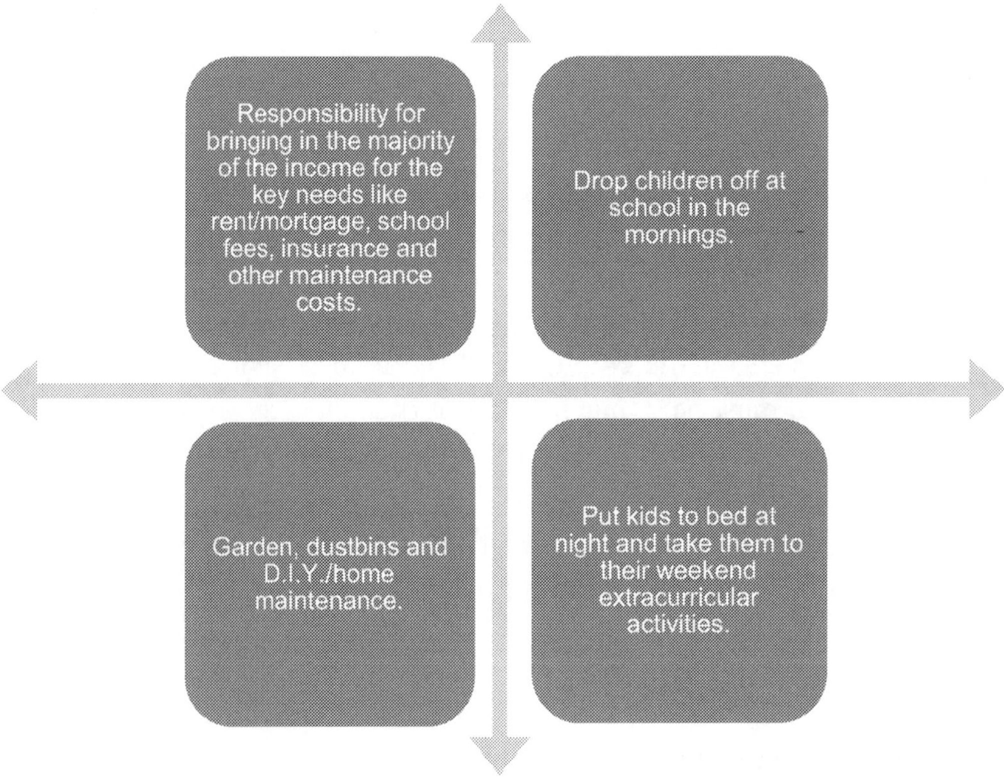

For Wives:

- Responsibility for managing the home
- Supplementing husband's income
- Housework

- Looking after the children

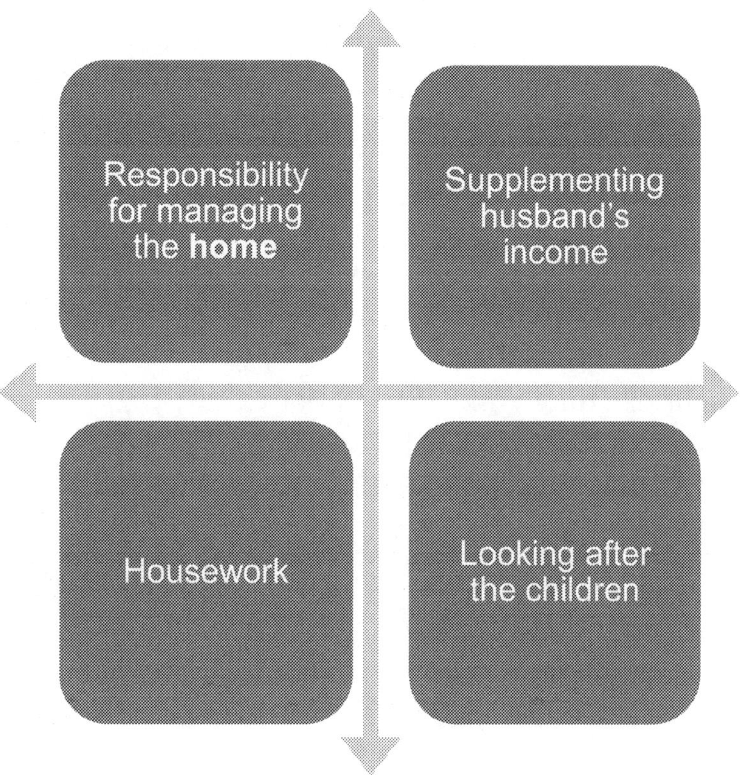

Conclusion

Roles truly determine relationships, and a clear understanding of well-outlined roles will help you avoid criticism, conflicts, crises and marital disintegration.

Application Section

ROLES, THEY DETERMINE RELATIONSHIPS, YOU KNOW

This Application Section consists of two parts: the individual section and the interactive section. Make sure you have enough time to interact with each other during the interactive section

Individual (Spouse) Section

Set the scene: Remain together as a couple, but complete this section on your own.

Goal: To gain knowledge about yourself as a reflection of God

Directions: Get a pen and paper and write your answers to these questions.

1. Husbands, are there tendencies you have noticed in your wife that you think she needs protecting from? How have you addressed them?
2. Husbands, think of two ways in which you can initiate love and sacrifice for your wife.
3. Wives, what do you do when you disagree with your husband? (Eph. 3:31)
4. Do you and your spouse have an understanding on how often you have sex?
5. In your marriage, who initiates sex? One spouse, or both of you? What are your expectations of each other?
6. Husbands, list six things, in order of priority, that you expect from your wife, noting which ones you are flexible about and those you are firm on.
7. Wives, list six things, in order of priority, that you expect from your husband, noting which ones you are flexible about and those you are firm on.
8. When did you determine these expectations – while you were dating, when you got engaged, or after you got married?
9. Is there anything you would like to change/incorporate?

Interactive (couple) section

Set the scene: Couple to stay together in a private area to talk freely.

Goal: To gain knowledge about each other, and your vision and view of the purpose of your marriage.

Directions: As well as discussing your answers together from the above section, discuss these points below.

1. Does the wife make **any** decisions for the family? Discuss.
2. Think of one occasion when you and your spouse could not agree on how a decision was to be made. How was it resolved?
3. In an ideal world, how would you and your spouse like the income for the family provided? Provided by one spouse? By both? By whom? Discuss.
4. Make a comprehensive list of household tasks, not leaving out even those things that you know are controversial for your spouse. Discuss who should do what, or who already does what.

Answers to Chapter 2

1. roles, responsibilities
2. equals
3. leader
4. servant
5. relationship
6. fellowship
7. breadwinner
8. listened
9. respect
10. responsibility
11. exemplify
12. protect
13. family
14. wolves
15. missing
16. appreciate
17. emulate
18. directing, esteem, sexually, holistic
19. obedience
20. help, support
21. decision-making
22. submit
23. respect, honour
24. intimacy
25. cohabit
26. Management
27. EXPECTATIONS
28. conflict

Chapter 3

DECISIONS, DECISIONS

Chapter Overview

- *The picking of a life-partner is, without a doubt, one of life's top three decisions, probably only ranking behind the decision to give one's life to Christ.*
- *Making a decision on inconsequentials like what colour clothes to wear and which route to take to work today do not hold a candle to reaching an outcome on whom to live with forever, have children with, and carry out life's other vital functions with.*
- *The commonest reason people give for getting married is 'We love each other!' Usually though, what people describe as love is either infatuation, a strong attraction or purely and simply lust.*
- *There can never be a one-size-fits-all formula for finding a spouse.*
- *Marriage involves the spirits, souls and bodies of the two people involved in it (1 Corinthians 6:16–17 GW).*

Lessons When Choosing a Life Partner:

For men

(a) A man should only seek a wife at the place where he gets his ________ nourishment, usually, but not confined to, a local assembly. It could, however, be any part of the Kingdom, any part of the Body of Christ.

(b) A man is to marry a woman who knows her own ____________.

For women

(a) No woman is to marry a man who does not have an intense, active, ____________

____________ with the God and Father of our Lord Jesus Christ, through Him, the Son.

(b) Ladies, a man who knows how to place things in their proper ____________ is an invaluable asset as a ____________ and a ____________ in the home.

(c) No woman should marry a man who has no ____________, ____________, ____________ or ____________.

Other lessons to note

1. It is ____________ who determines when a believer is ready to get married.
2. We are only to marry from our Father's family and from our spiritual relatives. We can under no circumstances marry anyone who does not share our ____________ (2 Corinthians 6:14–18 AMP).
3. In Bible typology, ____________, which is vital for life, for sustenance, for slaking one's thirst, is a picture of the ____________ (John 15:3, Ephesians 5:26, John 3:5, Titus 3:5c).
4. ____________ ____________ is a crucial part of any relationship. In fact, it is usually the first thing one encounters before one gets to know the person's character, spirituality and capabilities of intellect, emotion or will.
5. We must endeavour never to lose our physical appeal to our spouses, even with the passage of time.
6. Good dietary habits, exercise and taking time with one's appearance and hygiene are therefore lifelong essentials
7. Every believer is to marry a ____________.
8. A believer who has repented and turned away from immorality, and consecrated their lives to ____________ ____________ and celibacy till marriage, is restored by God and deemed a virgin.
9. We are not to marry a so-called believer who has not learnt to possess his vessel in ____________.
10. In Genesis 24:14, 44, the servant stated, 'she that thou hast appointed' and 'the woman whom the Lord hath appointed out for my master's son…'
11. In the first reference, the Hebrew word used for the phrase is '__________' which literally means 'whom Jehovah has appointed'.
12. In the second reference, the Hebrew word used is ***yakach*** which means 'to be right'.
13. ____________ are easier when men stay on the path of truth.

14. __________ makes you faithfully do everything written in the Book.
15. Isaac 'lifted up his eyes, and saw'. This, in the realm of the spirit, means he had __________.
16. Vision, apart from being the act or power of sensing with the eyes, is also the act or power of anticipating that which will or may come to be: which is also called __________________.
17. The man sees the ________ not the problem, the woman sees her ________. Yes, she must have a vision, but it must be submitted to her husband just as his is submitted to Christ.
18. __________ is a virtue vital to a good wife. Many ladies today, upon seeing their potential Isaacs, expose their cleavage, their thighs, their breasts, and any other physical asset.

The Checklist Before Saying 'I Do':

1. <u>Feelings and Emotions</u>

   > For a marriage to be successful in the long term, there must be mutual physical attraction.
   > In addition to loving your partner, you must also like them.

2. <u>Character Traits</u>

   > Are you content to marry the person just as they are?
   > Do their ________ values align with yours?

- Do they have glaringly irritating ________ or ________ that you absolutely cannot abide?
- Do you trust your intended partner? Are they trustworthy?
- Do they keep their ________, and is their word their bond?
- If not, do not go ahead with the marriage!

3. Education, Intellectual and Cultural Interests

- Education is one of the fastest and surest ways of advancing your economic status.
- Is your potential spouse apt to teach and teachable?
- Are they formally or informally ________? Inadequate motivation to grow and learn, unless shared by both partners, will lead to frustration and divorce.
- A couple that shares recreational, cultural and intellectual pursuits is more likely to stay together than a divergent duo.
- 'Can two walk together, except they be agreed?' (Amos 3:3).

4. Vocation

- No woman should marry a man who is not gainfully ________ or successfully running his own ________.
- For some women, work is crucial to their sense of well-being, emotional satisfaction and identity. Such a woman, marrying someone who wants a full-time home-maker, is faced either with the compromise of a part-time job or a home-based business. Otherwise, the marriage is doomed before it even takes off.
- Women, you may also want to bear in mind that a sole or principal provider may not always be able to provide or may not always be there; what happens to you then?

5. Family, Friends and Emotions

- God did not ask us to abandon our parents or neglect our ________ towards them. You marry into and unite two families when you tie nuptial bonds. Our relationships with our families invariably affect those with our spouses.

- The way a man treats his mother and sisters is a ________ to how he will treat his wife.
- The way a woman ________ to her father and other authority figures in her life tells a story that is relevant.
- ________ family issues, emotional baggage from the past, family traditions and culture can all be ________ to a happy marriage.
- In addition, your spouse's ________ tell you the most about who they really are. While we cannot choose our family, we certainly determine who we want to hang out with.

6. <u>Life Goals</u>

- What do you want to ________ after marriage and in the latter part of your lives?
- Questions around children must be asked: yes, no and how many, if any. What about if we cannot have children? Is adoption an option?
- Assess your partner's aspirations, continuing self-development and educational goals, and how they align with yours.
- What about the contributions you both hope to make to the welfare of the wider society?
- What giftings and graces do you both possess, and how do you intend to use them?

7. <u>Spiritual Perspective</u>

- Spiritual implications are priority.
- Is your partner ________ and ________ spiritually?
- Are they part of a local ________ where they are known, accountable, and working to help the visionary fulfil the Church's calling?
- The Multiple Witness Principle or the so-called 'Witness Protection Programme' (WPP) introduces a Biblical principle for establishing truth and how this can be used for determining whether God is involved in a relationship or not.

IV) The eternal principle

- 1st Example: Jesus stresses, 'If thy brother shall trespass against thee, go and tell him his fault between thee and him alone: if he shall hear thee, thou hast gained thy brother. But if he will not hear thee, then take with thee one or two more, that in the mouth of two or three witnesses every word may be established.'

> 2nd Example: For a second witness, we must turn to the story of the woman taken in adultery. After Jesus forgives the woman, He declares that He is the light of the world, and those who follow Him would not walk in darkness but would have the light of life. At this juncture the contentious, contemptuous Pharisees invoked this principle of two or three witnesses, saying, 'Thou bearest record of thyself, thy record is not true'. Jesus then corrected them by stating His authority to bear record to truth (He Himself being 'the Way, the Truth and the Life') John 14:6.
> 3rd Example: Jesus, however, goes further to quote the law in relation to His witness and to prove that He fulfilled its demands. For as He said, the Father bore witness of Him as much as He did of Himself (John 8:12–18). Further study will reveal that the Holy Ghost bears witness (John 15: 26–27); John the Baptist bore witness (John 5:33); the works that Jesus did bore witness (John 5:36); the heavens and the firmaments declare or bear witness to God's glory (Psalm 19:1); believers, past and present, also bear witness (Acts 1:8).

Practical Application of the Multiple Witness Principle or WPP

Step 1. Once a friendship has been entered into and mutual compatibility criteria established, it is time to go to God to seek His face on the matter. Using the checklist as a guideline, draw up a 'feasibility' table that contains the pros and cons of the relationship, the equivalent of a cost/benefit or a SWOT (________ ________ ________ ________ analysis.

Step 2. (Witness 1) Then take these issues to God and wait on Him till He speaks to you two or three times from His ________. His word will address either your concerns or flag up warnings that will serve as a deterrent (1 Samuel 16:7; Revelation 7:9).

Step 3. (Witness 2) Next you have to employ the services of one or two ________, ________ ________ or ________ who share your faith to pray along with you till they get a word or two from God's Word on your behalf. Whoever you choose is to share with you whatever word God gives them on your behalf, whether they understand it or not. It may be an answer to a query or issue you have raised of which they are unaware.

> Do not go to your pastor – he is too busy. Do not go to your best friend or closest sibling – they are usually too involved to be truly objective.

Step 4. (Witness 3) When all your scriptures are in, ask God to confirm what He has spoken at the mouth of an ________ ________, one with whom you have not discussed the issue. This serves as a control mechanism.

Beware of Idols in your Heart

- If you know what you want and want what you want and must have what you want, then be honest with yourself and just go for it, and be prepared to live with the consequences of your choice, good or bad (Galatians 6:7).
- The quality of one's decisions is based on the facts available, and we are so finite in knowledge, understanding and wisdom, it is best to let the Omniscient One help us in our decision-making.
- When we do it on our own, we lack the boldness and confidence to come to Him, let alone trust Him for a solution. We feel like we are being punished for our sins and are only getting what we deserve.
- Those, however, who wait on or trust in the Lord for help, will find new strength. It is written that 'only those people who are led by God's Spirit are His children' (Romans 8:14 CEV).

Conclusion

If the consent and involvement of earthly parents is of such importance, then how much more so those of our heavenly Father? If we give the reins of our relationships and marriages to the Almighty God, the galloping divorce rate, the rearing of marital disintegration, the neighing of neglect and the baying of domestic violence will all be tamed by our divine equestrian Master Trainer.

Application Section

DECISIONS, DECISIONS

This application exercise consists of two sections: the individual section and the interactive section. Make sure you have enough time to interact with each other during the interactive section

Individual (Spouse) Section

Set the scene: Couple to separate during this section.

Goal: To gain knowledge about your impending marriage and partner.

Directions: Get a pen and paper and write your answers to these next questions.

- Have you gone through the witness protection programme?
- If yes, what word have you received from this programme?
- If no, is this something you need to do before you get married?
- Are you absolutely assured that your wife- or husband-to-be is the right choice for you from God?

Interactive (couple) section

Set the scene: Couple to discuss this section together.

Goal: To gain knowledge about your choices made before you get married.

Directions:

- Do you have any doubts about your partner?
- Write out any pros and cons.
- Do any of the lessons for choosing a life-partner apply to you? Discuss these with your partner.

Homework

1. Go through the witness protection programme, if you as the future wife or husband have not already done so, and ensure you get a word from God for your impending marriage and spouse.

2. Read and meditate on these Bible passages: Daniel 7:9, 13, 22; 1 Corinthians 6:17 GW; 1 Corinthians 6:16 GW; 2 Corinthians 6:14–18 AMP; 1 Peter 2:9; John 15:3; Ephesians 5:26; John 3:5; Titus 3:5; Genesis 24:48; John 14:6; Genesis 24:27 AMP; Genesis 24:14, 44; Amos 3:3; Deuteronomy 19:15; Deuteronomy 17:1–6; Numbers 35:30; John 14:6; John 8:12–18; John 5:33; John 15: 26–27; Acts 1:8; 2 Corinthians 13:1; Genesis 41: 7, 8–15, 17, 22; Genesis 41:25; 1 John 5:5–6; 1 John 5:7; 1 John 5:8; 1 Samuel 16:7; Revelation 7:9; Ezekiel 14:1–4; Galatians 6:7; Romans 8:14 CEV.
3. For further counselling or to discuss your concerns on this matter, please speak to one of the volunteers or the course co-ordinator.

Answers to Chapter 3

1. spiritual
2. mind
3. personal, relationship
4. order, husband, leader
5. goals, ambitions, vision, a mission
6. God
7. faith
8. water
9. Word of God
10. physical attraction
11. virgin
12. sanctified sexuality
13. sanctification
14. Jeremiah
15. choices
16. meditation
17. vision
18. prophetic vision
19. provision
20. husband
21. Modesty
22. core
23. habits, beliefs
24. promises
25. educated

26. employed, business
27. responsibility
28. pointer
29. responds
30. Unresolved, detrimental
31. friends
32. achieve
33. growing, maturing
34. assembly
35. strengths, weakness, opportunities, threats
36. Word
37. friends, prayer partners, loved ones
38. independent witness

Chapter 4

COMMUNICATION

Chapter Overview

The secret to **any** successful relationship is effective ______________.

To walk with wisdom in your marital communication processes is to know when to __________ and when to ____________, to learn to listen beyond ____________ ____________, to realise that understanding is not always synonymous with agreement, to realise that not everyone has enjoyed the privileges you have had and to grasp the fact that while your marriage is private, it is a showcase for the world to marvel at.

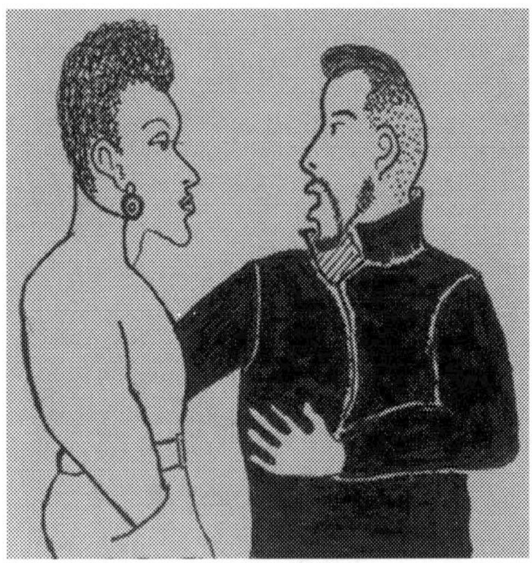

Communication: what is it good for?

Selwyn Hughes advises that if there is an invaluable insight couples are to begin their marriages with, it is to keep the ______________ lines open at all costs.

In Genesis 11, the people united in an objective: to build a city and a tower (the Tower of Babel) that reached heaven, and to make a name for themselves so they would not be scattered around the earth.

'The Lord said, if as one people speaking the same language they have begun to do this, then nothing they plan to do will be impossible for them' (Gen. 11:6 NIV).

Think of two achievements you have done, whether at work, home, in a hobby or activity, which were facilitated by effective communication:

1. ______________________________
2. ______________________________

'Me, Man; you, Woman.'

Men and women communicate in different ways. The differences do not make one way better than the other, just different, and the key is to allow for those differences and make the effort to understand each other.

_____________ in marriage and indeed other spheres of life depends on the ability of people to excel in the execution of the three components of effective communication.

List below the **three components of effective communication** discussed in the chapter:

a. ______________
b. ______________
c. ______________

For effective communication, we need to concentrate on the _____________ in order to understand what they are communicating. Communication is _____________ and _____________; in the former, you need to _____________ to what is being said.

Talking Exercise:

You and your spouse should sit down together. Pick a topic or issue you want to deal with. Think about it for a few minutes, then either talk about the topic/issue for a minute or write down what you want to communicate about that issue in three paragraphs that would add up to about one minute of reading, and read it out to your spouse.

When you have finished, reverse the roles so that your spouse talks about or reads a few paragraphs to you on another chosen topic/issue.

This exercise is just to utilise your talking skills.

Listening Exercise 1:

Your spouse should pick a topic or issue and talk about it for one minute. As your spouse is speaking, do **not** focus on what he or she is saying, let your mind wander and think about as many things, other than what your spouse is talking about, as you can within that one minute. When the minute is up, list to your spouse all the things you remember thinking about during that minute.

You and your spouse should reverse the roles and try this exercise again.

How easy or difficult was it **not to listen** to your spouse?

Listening Exercise 2:

Your spouse should sit down, pick a topic and start talking about it. Walk out of the room as they are talking and go to the room in your apartment/house furthest away from them. Walk around in that room for 30 seconds and then go back to the room where your spouse is; they should continue talking until you return to the room.

How difficult or easy was it to walk away from the conversation and not listen to what was being said?

In the two listening exercises above, it might have been easy **not to l**isten to what your spouse was saying (not because of who your spouse is, but because listening requires some degree of ________________ and active ________________

It is possible for background information (for example a film or TV programme, a radio programme or music) to wash over you, passively, especially when you have heard it before; however, even new information can wash over you, without you taking in the information, except for certain parts here and there which engage your attention. Listening to what someone is saying requires you to pay ____________ ____________, to focus and to put effort into comprehending the message being delivered. We invest this effort and focus when we are receiving instructions about tasks, work, banking, voting, buying a house and other such endeavours so we get the best result. Likewise, we need to invest this effort and focus in ____________ ____________ in order to get the best results.

Understanding Exercise 1:

Think back to a class or presentation you were in where you took notes. Did taking notes help you understand and retain what was said?

Understanding Exercise 2:

Now, think about a conversation you had where you repeated back to the other person what they had said, either to confirm or clarify a point. Did this action help to increase your understanding of the message that was being delivered?

Exercise:

As you have read in this chapter and probably observed for yourself, men and women communicate in different ways.

Given these gender differences in the approach to communication, think about how your spouse communicates with you.

1. Is there something about their communication style you like?
2. Is there something you would like them to work on?

Discuss your answers to these two questions. Decide if the answer to the second question is something your spouse can work on and improve, or something that is part of them that you can try to adapt to.

The key to initiating a good ____________ is having a genuine interest in your partner and their welfare. This will encourage you to discover the things that are of interest to them, and to concentrate your conversation on these things.

A key to initiating good conversation is ________ ________ ________ ________.

Exercise:

You and your spouse should consider the following questions which appeared in the chapter:

- When I make my spouse angry, do I always know why?
- Do I always know when my spouse is interested in making love?
- Are we perfectly matched as far as our sexual needs and desires are concerned?
- Do work, sports, television, children and family interfere with my ability to talk to or be with my spouse?

Come up with answers to the questions. When you are done, discuss your answers with each other. Do you agree with each other's answers?

If you do not, discuss further in order to identify the reasons for the differences in your perceptions.

'I was trying to protect you...'

Sometimes, one person in a marriage withholds important information from the other. Sometimes they do this to __________ ________, __________ __________ ________, or avoid ________.

Exercise:

Think of a time when you have withheld information from your partner for one of the reasons above or for a similar reason. Then answer the following questions-

- ❖ Did you achieve your aim?
- ❖ Did you regret withholding the information?
- ❖ If there were no negative repercussions to yourself from this action, do you think it was the **right thing** to do or the **safe thing** to do?
- ❖ How would you feel if the same was done to you?
- ❖ In a situation other than a marital one, for example work/friendship/hobby/ parent-teacher/ extended family or other scenario, how would you feel if you found out some information had been kept from you which others were privy to?
- ❖ Discuss this issue with your spouse. What did you both agree on?

Your spouse is meant to be the person you can be completely open with. This means you can be ______________ **and** ________________ with them.

Exercise:

Discuss with your spouse:

1. Do you think you always have to appear strong to your spouse?
2. Do you think your spouse will have a poor opinion of you if they see you in your weak moments? Or can this just remind both of you that you are human and the only 'super' person is God, who is our strength?

Is silence ever golden?

Matthew 12:35–37.

It is important to **always** keep the ____________ of communication open and keep talking, even (and especially) when things are difficult between you and your spouse. However, you have to make sure you **speak with the love you feel for them**. After all, you vowed to take care of each other and one way you can do that is by helping and not harming with your words.

James 1:19–20: 'Wherefore, my beloved brethren, let every man be swift to hear, slow to speak, slow to wrath: For the wrath of man worketh not the righteousness of God.'

Exercise:

Please note that this is a learning exercise aimed at helping you improve your communication and not to focus on past mistakes.

You and your spouse should sit down together. Each of you should think of two times when the other person said something that hurt you.

- Tell each other what those two things were and **why** they hurt you. Was it the words, the tone, the physical gestures, or all of these factors that made the communication hurtful?
- What can they do next time to ensure a constructive and not destructive interaction?

Here are a few handy tips from the chapter to make you a good listener and therefore a better communicator. Refer back to the chapter for details on these tips:

Tips for being a good listener and therefore a better communicator:

- **Listen to the complete message**
- **Work at listening skills**
- **Judge the content, not the form of the message**
- **Weigh emotionally-charged language**
- **Eliminate distractions**
- **Think efficiently and critically**
- **Learn to read between the lines**
- **Listen for the four sides of every message**

A few **barriers to effective listening and free-flowing communication** are:

- Self-centredness
- Inflexibility
- Naïveté
- The ostrich complex
- Stubborness and pride
- Judging words and feelings
- Semantics

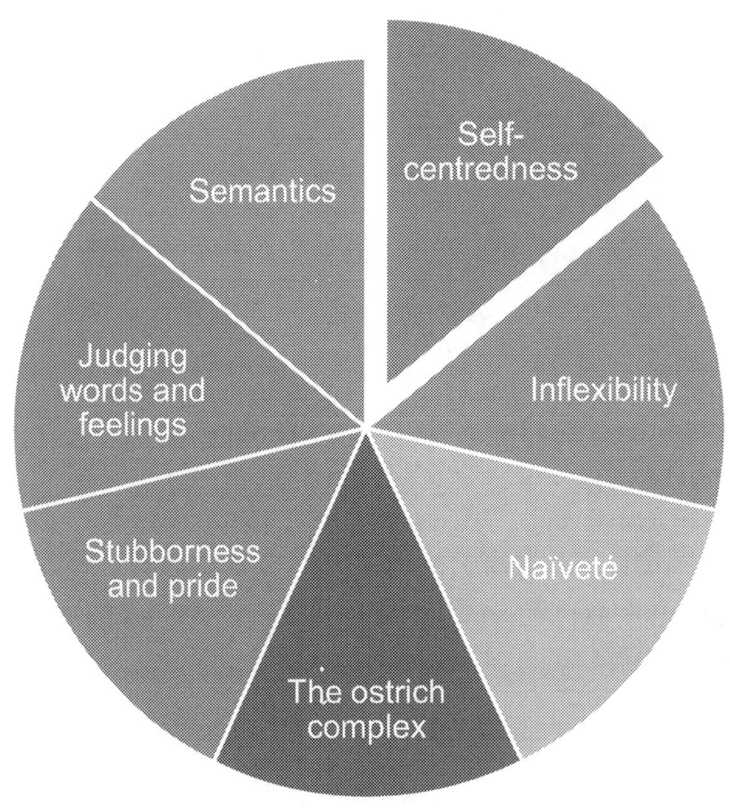

Below is a checklist from the chapter for the receiver in a communication interaction to be mindful of. Be careful about different perceptions and meanings that various people attach to the same word:

Checklist for the Receiver

- What are the messages in the signal?
- Which was the main message?
- Does the signal contain implicit messages?
- Was the signal congruent or incongruent?
- What was expressed on the level of meta-communication?
- Have you picked up the signal with four ears or with only one ear?
- Do I interrupt and never let my spouse finish what they are saying? If so, what drastic steps can I take to rectify the situation, like putting my hand over my mouth literally?
- Am I giving my undivided attention to my spouse maintaining eye contact, and shutting out distractions like the television, a quick glance at a newspaper, or finishing a chore?
- Did I let go of my own agenda by listening without planning my response?
- Am I mind-reading, rehearsing, filtering, judging, day-dreaming, advising, sparring, being right, changing the subject and placating?
- Do not give advice unless it is requested!

Exercise:

You and your spouse should each think of three short statements but do not reveal them to each other, for example 'I need to wash the car today.' Then communicate to your spouse, **by miming actions with no words or sounds**, what that statement is. It might seem silly, but think of it as playing a round of the party game 'charades'.

You have **50 seconds** to mime each short sentence. When you are done with your three statements, it is your spouse's turn and they should do the same with their sentences.

- Did you get the statements right?
- How easy or difficult was it to communicate your statement to your spouse?
- How easy or difficult was it to get the message being **sent to you**?

Note: With the exercise above, you were actively trying to understand the **intentional** body language of your spouse in order to correctly interpret the message they were sending to you.

Sometimes, the non-verbal messages we are sending are **involuntary** but can provide real insight into what the *real message* of our communication is.

Exercise:

1. Try and think of a time when you **unintentionally** gave something away in your mannerism whilst communicating with your spouse.
2. Try and think of a time when you **intentionally** used **subtle physical communication** to communicate a message to your spouse which was in some way **different** from what you were actually saying with your **words**. Did you expect them to understand what you were really communicating through your subtle physical actions because of how well they know you, and the intimacy you share? If they failed to get the point, did you have to put more **overt** effort into the physical actions to make sure your true message reached them?

Understanding

'Wisdom is the main thing; get wisdom; and with all your getting, get understanding' (Proverbs 4:7 MKJV).

If the fear of the Lord governs, for example, your marital communication, your foundation is solid and what you build will be lasting.

At the pinnacle of the ladder of marital success is wisdom. Wisdom is the practical application of knowledge and understanding for the advancement of the Kingdom of God, your personal lives and the lives of those around you.

Homework

You and your spouse should sit down next to each other in a quiet room, just the two of you and with no distractions (leave the TV and music off and put the books, newspapers, and to-do lists away). Neither of you should speak. Just spend **five minutes**, seated next to one another, in comfortable silence.

Note:

The aim of this exercise is to allow the two of you to spend time with each other. In our busy lives, whenever a couple see each other, they usually try to communicate about a task that needs to be completed or make some arrangement, for them or for their children. This exercise is meant to be about you and your spouse **just being next to each other**, in silence. It can be nice to enjoy each other's company without requesting or requiring anything from one another; **and** without it being under the heading of 'watching TV together'.

Answers to Chapter 4

1. communication
2. speak
3. listen
4. spoken words
5. communication
6. Success
7. talking
8. listening
9. understanding
10. speaker
11. verbal
12. non-verbal
13. listen
14. concentration
15. effort
16. consistent attention
17. marital communication
18. dialogue
19. asking the right questions
20. spare feelings, protect the spouse, confrontation.
21. strong, weak
22. lines

Chapter 5

LEARNING TO FIGHT PROPERLY

Chapter Overview

- Conflict resolution is one of the most important topics a couple have to come to grips with.
- Since it is inevitable that spouses who spend so much time together will argue and fight, it is imperative that from the very onset, they devise and agree on healthy conflict-resolution strategies, and fair fighting techniques.

Mnemonic acronym to enable couples internalise some simple rules for fair fighting:

FIGHT FAIR PLS

FIGHT

1. **_______________ is inevitable/inescapable**

   - The bottom line is that with every relationship, ________ is inevitable, and fighting is inescapable.

- A conflict is the product of two or more people coming into ________ or ______________.
- Conflict is the situation arising when differences between people remain __________.
- In marriage, many factors account for conflicts. The primary one is the little-recognised fact that men and women are ________ _____ ________: they look, think, speak and act differently.
- At the root of all conflicts is ________ and until the nature of Christ subdues the old man, the original ________ nature, ________ will continue to cause contention.
- _____________ is sure and ___________ guaranteed; it therefore behoves wise couples to utilise them for their personal and marital good.

2. Ignore distractions

- Usually _____________ or ______________ cause arguments that disguise the real problem.
- Try to be objective even when passions are strong.
- Assess what ____________ and ________ are motivating your behaviour.

3. Guard Your tongue

- Our ___________ hold the power of life and death (Proverbs 18:21).
- Abusive or acerbic assertions, ridicule and rancorous rantings, swearing and sarcastic statements and name-calling must be avoided as they attack your spouse's ______________.
- Once a person's character is under attack they become _________ and start looking for ways to counter your statements rather than listen to you.

4. Hang the history

- Focus on the ____________ ___________.
- 'You always…', 'Why don't you ever…?', 'You never…' are all examples of raking up history.
- Raising past ________ suggests to your spouse that nothing is new and nothing will ever change.

5. Tackle the conflict, not each other

- No matter what, husband and wife must stay on the same side of the fence because they are on the same team (Mark 3:25; Galatians 5:15).
- ________ is the chief reason why we lash out at each other in a fight.
- The chief cause of frustration is an inability to pinpoint the problem.
- Resist the temptation to highlight your partner's weaknesses and character flaws.
- The goal of an argument or conflict is to solve a ________. If you suppress your feelings, therefore, your spouse is not motivated to solve the problems they are unaware of.

FAIR

1. Face each other and hold hands

- Looking into each other's eyes as you attempt to resolve issues requires a ___________ that goes beyond your hurts and challenges.
- Holding hands softens the heart and unleashes a vulnerability that is mutual – as neither party towers over or talks down to the other.
- Facing each other means we cannot indulge in the perverse pleasure of slamming the phone or the door, or making a dramatic exit while shouting some unwholesome comment and trying to have the last word.
- Facing each other and holding hands highlights a commitment to shutting everything (television, radio, newspaper) and everyone else out because your spouse is more important and the things that touch them, touch you.

2. Anger must be controlled

- Unrestrained ___________ is one of humanity's most destructive emotions.
- Anger, like most other emotions and indeed virtually anything on earth when utilised properly, can be an instrument of ________ ________, ________, ___________ and ___________.
- Anger is a lot like temporary ________. When in the throes, many of us are capable of using a verbal hit-list on our mates we wouldn't think of using on a mugger. Threats! Maledictions! Name-calling!

Anger moves us to action when change is required in our lives. But the Bible strongly warns against unshackled anger.

 ***Ecclesiastes 7:9; Proverbs 13:10; Proverbs 14:17; Proverbs 29:22***

Here are six anger-management and stress-relief tips proffered by experts on About.com (Stress Management – www.offtherailskids.com).

- Examine your beliefs
- Eliminate some of your 'anger triggers'
- Develop effective communications skills
- Take care of yourself
- Employ handy stress-relievers
- Get support if you need it

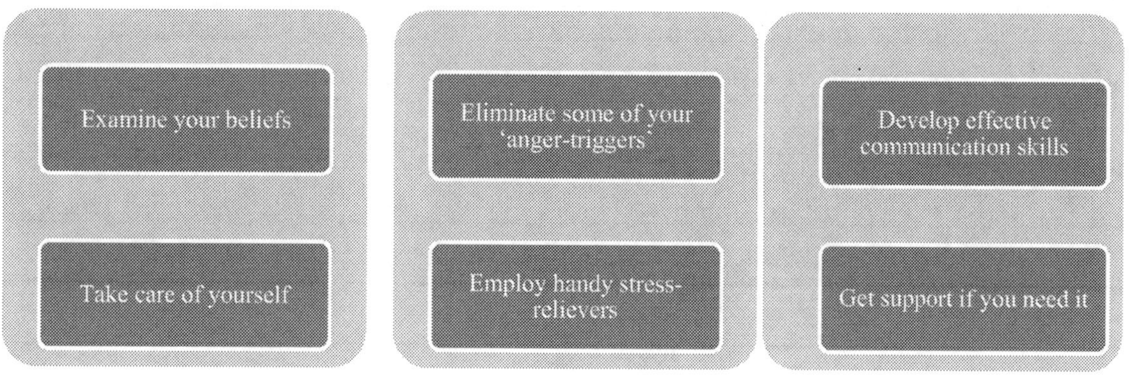

3. **I forgive you; please forgive me!**

- _____________ is at the very heart of Christianity and is the key to successful co-existence with other human beings.
- _____________ teaches you to forgive; _____________ gives you ample daily opportunities to practise what you have learnt.
- Forgiveness is not an issue of the emotions but of the ___________; it has nothing to do with how you feel, what you want, how you are perceived, or even who is involved. You forgive simply because God tells you to, and therefore that makes it the right thing to do.
- Forgiveness also does not wait for the recipient to repent, change, or even recognise their wrong.

- Forgiveness does not pretend the ____________ never happened, yet it does not focus on it.
- Forgiveness is bearing the brunt of someone else's ____________ and absolving them of every ____________.
- Born of ________ ________, forgiveness is a divine quality, injunction and characteristic.

4. Resolution techniques

- James Fairfield, a Christian marriage guidance counsellor, teaches five ways of resolving marital challenges:

  a. The first one, which is rooted in pride, is ________ __ _ ________. It is therefore more concerned with the end result, i.e. winning the argument, than how it affects one's partner and the marital relationship.
  b. The second one is ________. When your spouse is strong, forceful, aggressive and domineering, it is not uncommon for you to be a chronic 'withdrawer', especially if you have a more introverted or quiet personality type.
  c. The third technique is ____________.
  d. The fourth technique is to ________. The basic differences between compromise and yielding is that the former is a negotiation, while the latter is a capitulation. Yielding is the exact opposite of winning at all costs.
  e. The fifth, proper and most effective technique is to ______ __ ______.

1. Your personality type and the environment you grew up in are the two major factors that determine which technique you will gravitate towards.

2. Since most of our learning is by observation and 'osmosis', we tend to adopt the conflict-resolution style of the key authority figures in our lives – eg. parents, grandparents, guardians.

3. It is also not uncommon to have different strategies at different times or phases in our lives.

PLS

1. Problems Require Solutions

- You have to be willing to shift your focus from the problem to the ____________ ____________.
- Next, ________ and come up with potential solutions from each individual's perspective.
- You must be willing to change your individual behaviour for the marital or collective good.
- Each spouse must be willing to work on their character and personality, flaws, defects and shortcoming, and leave their partners to work on theirs.

Prescriptive problem-solving outline by Selwyn Hughes:

a. **The conflict between us is ____________.**
b. **Its effect on me is ________________.**
c. **My contribution to this conflict is ____________.**
d. **My proposed solutions are 1 ________ 2________ 3________ 4________ 5________.**
e **The agreed mutually accepted solution is ____________.**
f. **The change(s) I have to make is (are) ____________.**

(a) The conflict between us is ....

(b) Its effect on me is ....

(c) My contribution to the conflict is ....

(d) My proposed solutions are ....

(e) The agreed, mutually accepted solution is ....

(f) The change(s) I have to make is (are) ....

- Partners learn to take responsibility for their part in any conflict. This means they are less defensive and therefore forestall or eliminate their partner's offensive, and invite resolution rather than dissolution.

2. Learn to say sorry

- Most of humanity hates to be wrong and behave as if they never are. The root cause of this is ____________, which is the cause, consequence and bane of all interpersonal and divine relationships.
- Learning to ______________ when one has erred is a social skill that must be acquired quite early in the human cycle of development.
- Saying sorry is also a way of taking responsibility for your actions while considering other people's feelings.
- ____________ is recognising that there is a fault and it is yours, apologising for the fault, and accepting the forgiveness that follows with a genuine change of heart and a commitment to a new course of action.

The Bible actually teaches that without repentance, man cannot be reconciled to God – so you do have to say you are sorry.

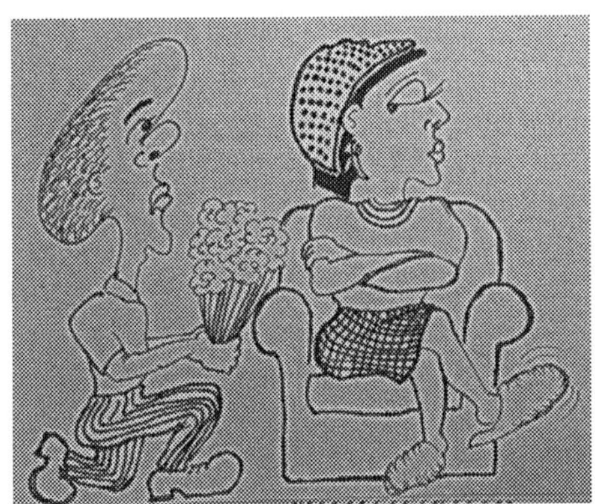

3. See the fight through

Some vital truths, and practical steps to resolving conflict:

- Conflict is common to, and inevitable in, all marriages.
- It would be unrealistic to expect a conflict-free marriage.
- Learn to approach conflicts appropriately when they occur.
- The choices we make during a conflict will lead either to isolation, or reconciliation and growth.

- If you have to take ten or so minutes to cool off, do so. Then come back to the issue and resolve it constructively.
- Ask yourself why you are angry, and cooperate with the Holy Spirit in bringing your anger under control before attempting to talk things through with your spouse.
- Be quick to forgive if you are the offended one, and to beg forgiveness if you are the 'perpetrator'.
- Lastly, remember as a team that you are both on the same side. Your spouse is not your enemy, even when there is a major conflict. Most of all 'you can (still) walk hand-in-hand even when you don't always see eye-to-eye'.

So the next time a conflict situation arises, as it inevitably will at some point, remember to:

FIGHT FAIR PLS.

Vital points to note:

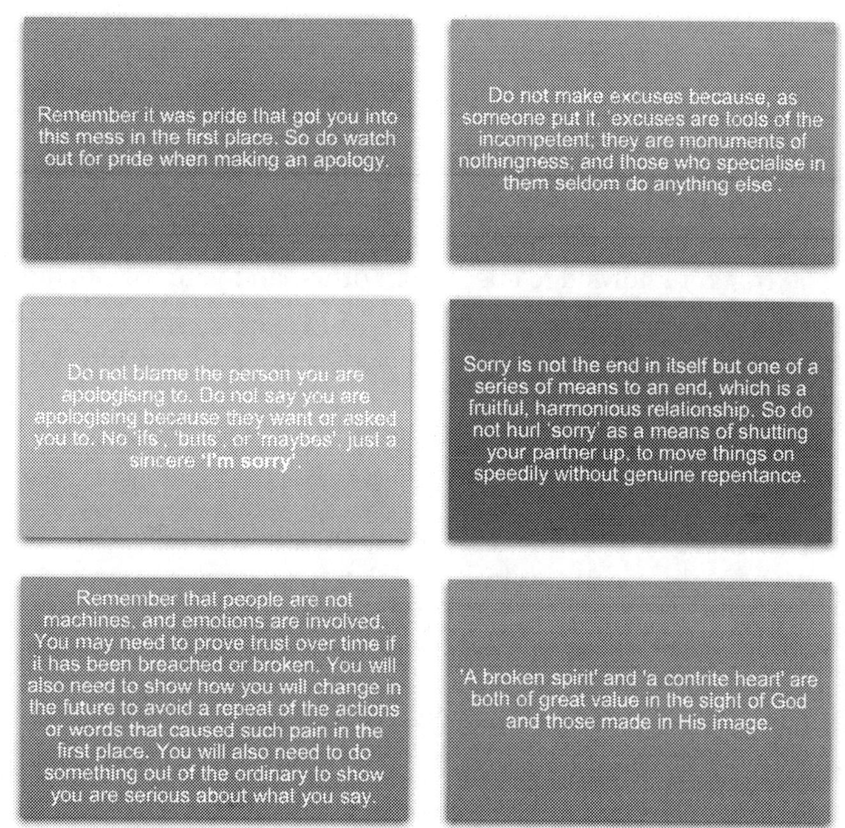

Application Section

LEARNING TO FIGHT PROPERLY

This application exercise comprises two sections: the individual section and the interactive section. Make sure you have enough time to interact with each other during the interactive section.

Individual (Spouse) Section

Set the scene: Remain together as a couple, but complete this section on your own.

Goal: To gain knowledge about yourself as a reflection of God

Directions: Get a pen and paper and write your answers to these next questions.

1. Which of the conflict resolution techniques do you favour when trying to solve a marital problem?
2. How does your spouse respond during a conflict?
3. Write down a conflict you feel has been left unresolved between you and your spouse.

Interactive (couple) section

Set the scene: Couple to stay together in a private area to talk freely.

Goal: To gain knowledge about each other, and your vision and view of the purpose of your marriage.

Directions:

1. Discuss your conflict-resolution techniques between yourselves.
2. Exchange your list of unresolved conflicts and discuss ways to resolve them using the conflict-resolution FIGHT FAIR PLS principles and techniques you have learnt in the class. Acknowledge your own faults in the conflict.
3. Do either of you need to, and are you willing to, apologise to each other for the conflict and your role in it?
4. Look into each other's eyes and taking turns; truly apologise, and ask for forgiveness from your spouse for any offence during the conflict.

Homework:

Read and reflect on Ephesians 4:26–27.

Answers to Chapter 5

1. Fighting
2. conflict
3. collision, disagreement
4. unresolved
5. different by design
6. pride
7. Adamic
8. pride
9. Conflict
10. fighting
11. Events, Issues
12. attitudes, beliefs
13. tongues
14. character
15. defensive
16. current conflict
17. offences
18. frustration
19. problem
20. commitment
21. anger
22. positive change, justice, equity, progress
23. insanity
24. forgiveness
25. Christianity
26. marriage
27. will
28. transgression
29. misdemeanour
30. indebtedness
31. *agape* love
32. winning at all costs
33. withdrawing

34. compromise
35. yield
36. resolve the conflict
37. potential solutions
38. brainstorm
39. pride
40. apologise
41. Repentance

Chapter 6

PARENTS, IN-LAWS AND OUTLAWS!

Chapter Overview

- The commonest in-law problems are between the wife and her husband's mother.
- The issue of parents and in-laws requires great foresight, wisdom, and clear rules of engagement.
- In marriage, we promise to make our spouse the number one person in our lives. The difficulties with in-laws include, but are not limited to:

I. A parent-in-law showing favouritism to one grandchild over another;
II. A mother-in-law criticising her daughter-in-law's cooking or housekeeping skills;

  a. Asking when the couple are going to have children (very common amongst families of Afro-Caribbean descent);
  b. Unsolicited parenting and other advice;
  c. Criticising how the couple raise and discipline their children;
  d. Parents who always try to control their children;
  e. In-laws who simply won't let go of their children and let them grow up;
  f. The painful realisation that your parents and your in-laws will never get along;
  g. The concern about in-laws who do not share your faith and are having a negative influence on their grandchildren;
  h. In-laws who make you feel inadequate, unsuccessful and never good enough for their offspring;
  i. In-laws who have come to 'visit' and have instead given themselves an 'indefinite leave to remain' … and many more.

III. It is clear that the problems with parents and in-laws can unfold in innumerable permutations such as:

i. Father/mother and their ____________,
ii. Spouse and ________________;
iii. Spouse and ______ _________ ___ _________
iv. The two sets of _____________________.

IV. Selwyn Hughes advances four possible reasons for this:

a. Society is mainly _________________ and so women are forced to compete for the attention of men. A wife is thus in competition with her mother-in-law for her husband's affection.
b. The wife feels insecure and inadequate as she prepares for her new role, in which she has no experience, in competition with her seasoned mother-in-law.
c. The marriage of a child is far more threatening to a woman, who is primarily a home-maker, than to the father, who works away from home.
d. Men deal with conflicts differently from how women deal with them.

V. Guidelines for productive relationships between every couple (newly married or veterans) and their parents and in-laws.

A. '...And the two shall become one'

- There can be no ________ _________.
- A man must leave his father and mother, so there must initially be a literal geographical _______________.
- There must be a psychological breaking away from the old allegiances and authority structures as a new home, with a new head, new members and new rules, is born.
- The buck stops with the new husband who is the ______________ ________, ably assisted by his wife, the __________ _______________.
- A husband is a man with a backbone, which he uses, and he is thus unafraid to make decisions that affect him and his family.

> *'Your primary human relationship now is with your spouse, not your parents. Your commitment to God comes first; then your bond to your spouse; then to any children you might have; then to your family of origin; and then to extended family and friends.'*

- The importance your spouse's parents and siblings still have in his/her heart shouldn't be underestimated. But the influential role they once held in your joint decision-making is to change.
- Becoming '________ ________' refers of course to the joys of giving oneself to one's spouse in devoted and joyful abandon in the consecrated and God-ordained act of sex.

B. Good fences make good neighbours

- One of the commonest causes of in-law problems is an ________ __ ________ for dealing with parents and in-laws.
- Well-defined ___________ are crucial for letting parents and in-laws know when they are or are not welcome into your home or personal affairs.
- These boundaries must be discussed, negotiated and ratified by both spouses with the necessary degree of specificity and detail.
- You must never assume you and your spouse are on the same page until you have talked about the relevant details.
- It might be better to reach an agreement when you are engaged, as this will set the tone for expectations on all sides while laying a lasting foundation, even for when children come into the picture.

Part of the process of growing up and maturing enough to get married is your willingness to confront issues and people (and the bogeymen!) you could previously not confront, on account of your lack of understanding due to immaturity.

C. Boundaries to be set for in-laws

1. Your discussion with your spouse must also involve ___________ ________.

    - Constant phone calls also mean personal family details will invariably be shared.
    - Visiting families must have a valid return ticket, and their length of stay must be discussed and agreed upon by both husband and wife before the family member arrives.

2. Next you must set ___________ ___________.

   - This sets out the stipulation that all decisions are to be made by husband and wife without prior consultation with parents and in-laws.
   - Any subsequent disapproval by in-laws must NEVER result in a change of heart or direction by husband or wife unless by mutual reconsideration.

3. Set boundaries for the ___________ and ___________ of your children.

   - Your children are a God-given trust, and you and your spouse are responsible for bringing them up in the nurture and admonition of the Lord.
   - This means that you set the rules and regulations in your home and everyone who comes into your sphere of jurisdiction must abide by them whether or not they consider themselves older, more experienced and wiser than you.

D. Communicate your needs to your parents/in-laws

Once your boundaries have been set then it's time to talk to both sets of parents about them.

- Each partner holds their family in check.
- If a wife has a problem with her husband's parents, it falls to the husband to bring that issue before his parents whether or not it is convenient and comfortable, and the same applies if the tables are turned and the husband has issues with his in-laws.
- As a rule a child will have more ___________ with his or her own parents.
- We know best how to influence our biological parents, so we must use this grace to stoutly defend and uphold the rights of our spouse and nuclear family.
- Remember that your mother or father-in-law is different from your parents. You cannot compare the two because in most cases your in-laws will come up short.
- Remember that your parents are obliged to love you: they don't have much choice, and they have had decades of practice. Your in-laws, on the other hand, do not have the same obligations.

- Pick your battles, giving in on the inconsequentials and wisely and patiently negotiating the vital stuff.

It is also important, as much as lies within your power, to avoid using your spouse as a third party in the communication process. Speak directly to the troublesome in-law who hurt your feelings and try to resolve the issue. Do it as soon as possible and often you will discover that the problems are misunderstandings which can be easily and quickly resolved.

E. Practical tips for coping with difficult in-laws

a. Learn to control your ____________.

- The Preacher teaches that he that keeps his ____________ keeps his life.
- Be agreeable to any criticism your in-laws may throw at you and even shock them further by seeking their counsel to improve things. Remember, you do not have to carry out their instructions but you will have succeeded in defusing the tension and disarming them completely.
- Never criticise or complain about your spouse to his/her family.
- Never quarrel or fight in front of them, and never get drawn into sibling rivalry or any other existing family feuds.

b. Keep in touch with your ____________.

- At least once a week or fortnight, preferably at a set day and time, ring up your in-laws and enquire about their welfare.
- Agree to visit them with the children monthly. This serves several purposes:

  o Firstly, it satisfies their desire to see their offspring and their grandchildren;
  o Secondly, it means there will be reduced pressure for further socialisation opportunities;
  o Thirdly, repeated exposure makes people like things, faces, music, and even things they would normally not be drawn to, better.

c. Give them ____________ opportunities:

- Give your in-laws, particularly if they are retired or work from home, the opportunity to babysit sometimes.
- Be aware and responsive to '*grandparent privilege*'. Grandparents get to be indulgent, if they want. Or super-strict. Or have weird rules. It falls to parents, to restore the balance when the kids come home.
- However, and equally important, grandparents and in-laws must also respect '*parent privilege*' (the rights of parents to bring up their children as they deem fit).

d. Be respectfully ____________ when problems arise.

- The majority of relationship problems arise because one party assumes the other to be ________________.
- Your in-laws, unlike your parents, do not know how you feel and what you like or hate, unless you tell them, so educate them when necessary.
- Learn and apply assertive techniques to express how you feel.

Seven practical 'Coping Tips For New Parents' suggested by Jenna D. Barry in article 'Do Your In-laws Drive You Crazy?'

The next time your in-laws call to invite themselves over, you could say, 'Tomorrow won't work for me, but next Wednesday would be great if you're free then.'	• Giving an alternative date softens the perceived rejection.
If your in-laws show up unexpectedly, feel free to say, 'This isn't a good time for me, but you're welcome next Saturday evening. From now on, give us a call before you come over. I'd hate for you to waste a trip if we're unavailable.'	• If they ignore your suggestions, one expert suggests you don't answer the door next time they just 'happen to pass by'.
Be specific about the duration of visits to which in-laws are invited.	• For example, say 'We'd love for you to come and visit us between December 23rd and Boxing Day, if that works for you.' Or 'I'm available from midday to 2pm on Friday if you'd like to come over to the house.'
When in-laws offer unsolicited advice on issues such as which party to vote for, breast-feeding, breast pumps, best conception techniques and remedies;' or how to raise your children, hear them out patiently.	• Most times that is the end of the matter as they may not follow up to ensure you do things their way. If, however, they insist, or try to follow up on your core values and deeply-held convictions, then say: 'Thanks for your invaluable input, which has helped me put things in perspective. I have, however, decided to do it the other way instead.' • Giving the reasons will also help to defuse tensions and show that you are not just being contrary, arbitrary or difficult.

e. Should you, however, have in-laws from hell who try to manipulate you and lay a guilt trip on you for daring to have needs that differ from theirs, then you must stand your ground – or face a lifetime of sorrow and anguish of soul as they take control of more and more areas of your life. Some helpful tips/examples:

- 'You're entitled to your opinion (Helen), but this isn't up for negotiation.'

  - o Call your in-law by name, not 'mum' or 'Mrs Bloggs', as this will discourage their attempt at domination.
  - o Calling your in-law by name may not always work, especially in certain cultures, but the need to stand your ground is universal.

- 'I'm sorry you're upset (Harry/Dad), but I still insist that you call first before coming over.'

  - o You are thus acknowledging his dissatisfaction, but insisting you expect him to respect your needs nonetheless).

'For your marriage to succeed and you both to be happy, then these are vital issues to contend with. No doubt the greater onus is on the husband, who must grow up quickly and be willing to confront anything that affects the welfare of his family. If he thus sets a good example, his wife will not hesitate to follow suit.'

F. Two Is Company, Three's A Crowd (The TICTAC Rule)

a. Your marriage was designed by ____________ to be private and this explains the primary injunction to leave your father and mother and cleave to your wife, and to become one flesh. 'United we stand...'

b. The major reason why many parents and in-laws become intrusive is because they were invited in and given free rein in the first place.
c. Working with your spouse is the key factor.
d. A good ____________ and ____________ framework will stifle any attempt by an outsider to drive a wedge between you.
e. You must, however, never turn away from your partner to your parents in an attempt to resolve your marital issues.
f. Agree with your spouse on what specific information the family is to be privy to. Less is usually more!
g. Never place your spouse in the unsavoury and impossible position of choosing between you and their relatives.

VI. Give Thanks With a Grateful Heart

a. Giving thanks is a ____________.
b. Proper ____________ is a hard, demanding lifetime commitment that is often thankless.
c. Write letters of appreciation to your spouse's parents and their future in-laws, especially before marriage. This letter is to:

    - look back at all your parents or guardians have done to contribute to making you who you are today;
    - recognise physical and abstract benefits, educational and social advantages, moral and religious education.

d. The letter to your in-laws-to-be is to thank them for raising a gem, an asset and a source of pride.

    - Highlight the things that drew you to your bride- or groom-to-be, and what enamours you to them even now.
    - Where applicable, celebrate the length and success of their marriage and how it is an inspiration and a benchmark to you.

e. For those whose parents have been separated, or divorced and/or remarried, or not brought up by their biological parents, write separate letters to each of your parents as well as your guardian or foster/adoptive parents.

Application Section

PARENTS, IN-LAWS AND OUTLAWS!

This Application Section consists of two sections: the individual section and the interactive section. Make sure you have enough time to interact with each other during the interactive section.

Individual (Spouse) Section

Set the scene: Remain together as a couple, but complete this section on your own.

Goal: To gain knowledge about yourself as a reflection of God.

Directions: Get a pen and paper, and write your answers to these next questions.

1. Write down any current issues you are facing with your in-laws.
2. How do you think it should be resolved?
3. Have you discussed this issue and your suggested resolution with your spouse?

Interactive (couple) section

(Timing of this section to be included and discussed?)

Set the scene: Couple to stay together in a private area to talk freely.

Goal: To gain knowledge about each other, and your vision and view of the purpose of your marriage.

Directions:

1. Discuss the in-law issues and the resolution you have both agreed with each other.
2. Is this something you are both willing and ready to work on and accomplish together?
3. Do you need to have a discussion with your in-laws about the issues? Are you both willing and ready to do so?

Homework:

1. Plan to schedule an appointment and discuss any lingering issue or problem you have with your in-laws using the identified techniques in this workbook.
2. Agree to put your spouse first concerning any disagreement with your in-laws and your spouse.

Answers to Chapter 6

1. son/daughter
2. father-/mother-in-law
3. both sets of siblings
4. in-laws
5. male-dominated
6. divided loyalties
7. relocation
8. executive chairman
9. managing director
10. one flesh
11. absence of guidelines
12. boundaries
13. time boundaries
14. decision-making boundaries
15. welfare, discipline
16. credibility
17. tongue
18. mouth
19. in-laws
20. child-care
21. assertive
22. clairvoyant
23. God
24. communication, conflict-resolution
25. grace
26. parenting

Chapter 7

'I CAN'T LIVE WITHOUT YOU!'

Chapter Overview

- 'The biggest single __________ to a fruitful and joyous Kingdom-based marriage is attempting to meet your __________ __________ needs in and through your marriage partner.' (Selwyn Hughes)
- Man's three basic needs are for __________, __________ and __________.
- A godly, close-knit family unit is the best __________ to nurture in a child a healthy sense of security, significance and self-worth.
- Everybody has basic personal needs which are crying out to be __________.

MAN'S THREE MAIN BASIC NEEDS:

A. SECURITY

- Security is freedom from __________, __________ or __________.
- It is a need best met by being assured someone __________ you and is not only concerned with, but working for, your __________.

B. SIGNIFICANCE

- Significance means the sense of being __________.
- It is a yearning every individual has to be __________ to their particular environment by __________ positively towards its development, __________ their peculiar gifts, skills and callings.

C. SELF-WORTH

- The need for self-worth means a sense of one's ____________ or ____________ as an individual.
- It also has to do with self____________ and self____________ Ironically, a person's self-worth is actually determined by their ____________ of how other people value, esteem, respect or see them.

I. Out of these three basic needs come five of life's most important questions:

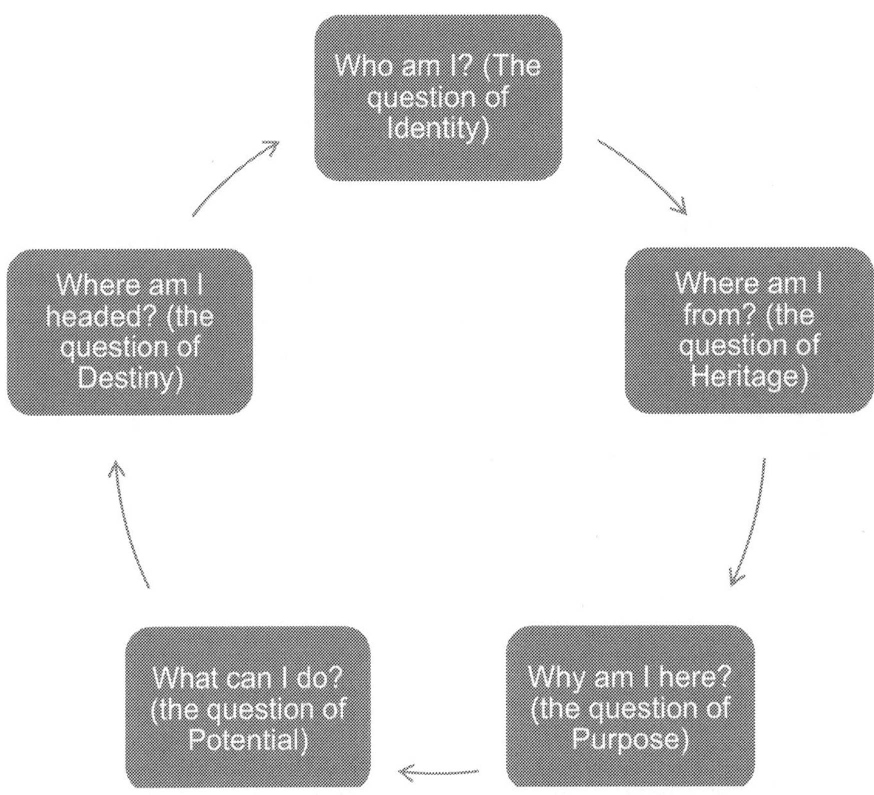

II. A home where the husband loves his wife even as Christ loves the Church, and the wife submits to his loving leadership as the Church does to Christ, will inevitably be a haven for raising ____________ children.

- Mothers too have lost their compassion and abandoned the nurture and care of their children as they pursue careers and 'filthy lucre'.

III. Two important facts to note at this point:

1. Fact one is that ____________ human being, including your good and esteemed self, has the ____________ to meet your basic personal needs. Adam's self-worth was boosted by God who blessed him, and empowered him with the power of fruitfulness, multiplication, replenishment, subjugation and dominion.

   - The devil's goal was to destroy man's ____________ to his true source. He succeeded in hijacking man's confidence in God's love, taking it from him, such that now everyone is born with inordinate levels of ____________;
   - This is further exacerbated by the negative influences of ____________ families, sexual ____________, paedophilia, poverty, crime, and other aspects of our prevalent contemporary malaise;
   - The escalating suicide rates, sometimes in the wealthiest communities and economies, testify to the loss of a ____________ of significance;
   - At the same time, the debasing activities and situations people allow themselves to dwell in are pointers to the prevalent lack of self-esteem.

2. The second fact is that due to these basic ____________ not being met, personality disorders may arise, such as: ____________, or ____________.

   - Frozen needs: Some of us enter adulthood with needs that were not adequately met in ____________, such as the needs for love, security and belonging. Often these early unmet needs freeze into ____________ behavioural patterns and enter our ____________ with us. Our adult behaviour is then based upon those basic needs from our childhood (Norman H. Wright);
   - Perfectionism: The striving for ____________ and the setting of excessively high ____________ standards, accompanied by overly ____________ self-evaluation, and concerns regarding others' evaluations.

Many people want to get married simply because they are literally dying to have their basic personal needs met.

IV. The void left in our lives since the fall of our first father, Adam, in the garden of Eden, is _________.

- Sex will not fill this ____________, alcohol will fall short, money, power, position and influence just will not make the mark, and definitely your spouse, children, family, friends, colleagues and acquaintances cannot bridge the yearning, yawning chasm. Only a personal ____________ with the Almighty God through His Son Jesus Christ will bring anyone to the place of ____________.
- Jesus told his disciples, who wanted to know the way to the place He was headed before His crucifixion, death, burial and resurrection, that He was the Way, the Truth and the Light, and that no man could gain access to the Father except by Him.
- Giving one's ____________ to Christ therefore becomes an essential ingredient for a ____________ life on the earth. This involves knowing Jesus and developing a deeper intimacy with Him through learning to be effective disciples of not just His words, but their effective implementation.
- Only such a person, who has matured sufficiently to be whole, is therefore qualified to take a spouse, and not be yoked to in a deadly, debilitating, parasitic relationship.
- Being ____________ and ____________ on Christ to meet their personal needs, couples are free to give ____________ love and ____________ to each other, and this is in part what God meant when He instructed that a man should 'leave his father and mother and cleave unto his wife and they (two) shall become one flesh'.

V. People referring to their spouses call them 'my better half'. This is erroneous on two levels:

- Firstly, a half is a half and so technically can neither be better nor worse than its other half.
- Secondly, God never expects two halves (a half man and a half woman) to come together to make a whole couple!
- Rather, two whole (complete in Christ) human beings come together to make an autonomous unit, a couple, one flesh.

IV. Expecting your spouse to ____________ you, ____________ you and bring you to self-actualisation means setting yourself up for ____________ and frustration. When you learn how to let God do this through your relationship with His Son, you take the pressure off your spouse and become an example they can emulate or aspire to as they see you mature.

Helpful hint: Stop telling your spouse you cannot live without them. They know it is not true, and it engenders cynicism and distrust. Tell them instead: 'I can live without you but I choose not to!'

Application Section

'I CAN'T LIVE WITHOUT YOU!'

This Application Section consists of two sections: the individual section and the interactive section. Make sure you have enough time to interact with each other during the interactive section

Individual (Spouse) Section

Set the scene: Remain together as a couple, but complete this section on your own.

Goal: To gain knowledge about yourself as a reflection of God.

Directions: Get a pen and paper and write your answers to these next questions.

- Can you identify ways where you have tried to get your spouse to meet any of your three basic needs?
- Do you think your spouse fulfilled those needs at that time?
- Do you understand how your spouse was unable to meet those needs?

Interactive (couple) section

Set the scene: Couple to stay together in a private area to talk freely.

Goal: To gain knowledge about each other, and your vision and view of the purpose of your marriage.

Directions: Spend this time discussing ways you may have put pressure on your spouse to meet your basic needs that can only be met by God.

Homework:

Spend your quiet time praying and reflecting on any unmet needs you are still dealing with, and ask God to meet those needs.

Answers to Chapter 7

1. obstacle, basic, personal
2. security, significance, self-worth
3. environment
4. met
5. danger, fear, anxiety
6. loves, welfare
7. important
8. relevant, contributing, utilising
9. value, worth
10. esteem, respect, perception
11. well-balanced
12. no, capacity
13. connection, insecurity
14. broken, abuse
15. sense
16. needs, perfectionism, exhibitionism
17. childhood, rigid, marriage
18. flawlessness, performance, critical
19. God-shaped
20. void, relationship, fulfilment
21. life, successful,
22. whole, dependent, unconditional, acceptance
23. validate, complete, failure

Chapter 8

DIFFERENT BY DESIGN

Chapter Overview

- For we are God's ________________, created in Christ Jesus to do works, which God prepared in advance for us to do' (Ephesians 2:10 NIV).
- There are notable differences between males' and females' DNA programming within their DNA from the moment of ________________.

A. Male/Female Differences

To ________________ your spouse into another 'you' is to ________________ the purpose for which they came into your life in the first place, and demonstrates lack of understanding of the purpose of your being joined to your spouse in holy matrimony.

Four Main Male/Female Design Differences:

i. ________________________________

ii. ________________________________

iii. ________________________________

iv. ________________________________

1. Physical Differences

- The average man is ______________ and ______________ and has more bodily ______________, especially on the chest and extremities, than the average woman.
- Women also have a different ______________ structure with a shorter head, broader face, less protruding chin, shorter legs and a longer ______________ than men.
- Women have greater ______________ ______________ than men, and in developed countries ______________ men by several years (four to eight in the United States of America).
- Women also have ______________ kidneys, liver, stomach and appendix. However, they have ______________ lungs and hearts.
- Men's higher levels of testosterone causes them to produce greater amounts of red blood cells. A woman's blood contains more ______________ and 20 per cent fewer red cells.
- 23 per cent of a woman's body is ______________, compared to 40 per cent of a man's.

2. Mental/ Emotional Differences

- Men will tend to define themselves by their ______________ and ______________, while women define their self-worth by the quality of their ______________.
- For women, relationships are crucial in a way that is inexplicable to men, while men talk about sports, work, the news, technology, cars and gadgets.
- The next major difference is that women are more ______________ than men: they take a deeper ______________ in people, feelings, and building relationships.
- Men are wired to see 'the big picture', the ______________ perspective, the macro level. Women, however, tend to zero in on the ______________, the minutiae, the micro level.

The area of greatest stress, misunderstanding and conflict, however, is the difference between how the two genders use words.

- Women use words to express ______________ and ______________, while men use words to convey ______________ and ______________.

- In addition, women think __________ and therefore use words to explore their __________, debate an issue, or cultivate and maintain relationships.
- Men, on the other hand, meditate on issues and tend to __________ only when they have reached a __________ or worked out a __________.

Women love to talk and on average speak 6,000 words a day, make 2,000 vocal sounds and 8,000 gestures, facial expressions, movements of the head and other body signals.

By contrast men speak less than half the total of a woman's words with 3,000 words on average, 1,500 vocal sounds and 2,500 body signals.

- Men have a mechanical ability to separate all of life's affairs into __________ like the pigeonholes for keys at a hotel reception. This means that work, sleep, sex, study, prayer, food and recreation are all __________ activities for men.
- Women, on the other hand, tend to be __________ and all their life's activities __________ and __________, one into another.
- Women need more time to adjust to __________, whereas men can __________ quicker. This explains why many single men frequently change jobs even when this entails moving to another town or country, and marvel at their wife's reluctance to move even once when they have married.
- Men are *donors*, women are *incubators.*
- Men are hunters/gatherers by nature, while women are nurturers and home-keepers.

Be very careful what you give to a woman because it will come back to you: 'good measure, pressed down, shaken together and running over' will she return to your bosom.

3. Intuitive differences

- Women possess a keen sense of __________ and an innate capacity to discern minute details and variations in the appearance, mood or demeanour of people they relate to. Add to this their 'wide-angled' peripheral vision, and their keener auditory and olfactory senses, as well as their superior communicative skills, and you can understand why they can perceive or feel what men cannot.

- That 'sixth sense', or 'female intuition', is the product of a woman's more finely tuned sensory skills.

4. Sexual Differences

- Using the image of batteries, men can be likened to the 'Ever Ready', while women are more like 'Duracell', which lasts and lasts.
- A man's sex drive is _______________, stronger and more straightforward than a woman's.
- A woman's sex drive is markedly _______________ than that of a man, and is more influenced by social and cultural factors.
- A man's sex drive can also be likened to a gas cooker which lights up instantly with a 'Whoosh!' and instantly operates at its optimum, while possessing a capacity to be switched off just as quickly. A woman's sex drive is more like hot coal or a hot plate which takes time to heat up, becomes red- or white-hot at its peak, then takes time to cool down again.
- A man needs little or no _______________ for sex. A woman, however, needs hours of _______________ and _______________ preparation. So when it comes to sex, a woman needs a reason, while a man needs an opportunity and a venue.

A woman's sex drive is influenced by occurrences in her life, whether small or great. Anything that induces stress in her life – sick, troubled or troublesome children, conflicts with friends or relations, job-related hassles, weather exigencies and many other such matters – render sex for women an unattractive unwanted proposition. The very opposite is true of men. In fact, sex is one of the tools married men utilise to dissipate tension, induce amnesia when all hell in breaking loose, or bring elusive sleep in time of crises.

Understanding the sexual differences between men and women

Men	Women
• Men are visual and stimulated by sight, and want sex as often as possible. • Most men are proactive with sex. • A man is ready in thirty seconds or less for sex, and once sex gets going it takes a healthy male about two and a half minutes to reach orgasm from when he starts. • A man hits his peak sexual performance level at age 19.	• Women are auditory and stimulated more by touch and romantic words than by what they see. • Most women are reactive with sex. • Psychologically and physiologically, a woman needs at least thirty minutes of foreplay before she is ready for sex, and it takes an average healthy female thirty minutes to reach orgasm. • A woman's sexual peak occurs between the ages of 36 and 38.

With all these vital clues to the design differences between men and women, every marriage should be better equipped to succeed. This is necessary, as ignorance is the single biggest factor responsible for the break-up of marriages.

Conclusion: One statement can be true of both sexes in diametrically opposite senses, because He who created them at the onset, male and female, made them different by design, yet united in purpose.

Application Section

DIFFERENT BY DESIGN

This Application Section consists of two sections: the individual section and the interactive section. Make sure you have enough time to interact with each other during the interactive section

Individual (Spouse) Section

Set the scene: Remain together as a couple, but complete this section on your own.

Goal: To gain knowledge about yourself as a reflection of God.

Directions: Get a pen and paper and write your answers to these next questions.

a. How do you communicate your sexual needs and desire to your spouse. Does it always get you the desired response? If not, do you need to change your methods?
b. Is your spouse always satisfied after sex?
c. Do you have any fears about sex? List them. How can your spouse assuage these fears?
d. Do you fully trust your spouse with your body and sexual needs?

Interactive (couple) section

Set the scene: Couple to stay together in a private area to talk freely.

Goal: To gain knowledge about each other, and your vision and view of the purpose of your marriage.

Directions: Complete the sentences below:

1. Leading up to sexual intimacy, I would like you to ______________
2. During sex I would like you to ______________
3. I am always very eager for sex when you ______________
4. I feel unenthusiastic sexually when you ______________

Homework:

A. Spend time together, praying about any sexual/intimacy issues you may have in your marriage.
B. Schedule a day and time, or a weekend, when you can both get away and have an 'alone time' away from the kids and family, for sexual communication and intimacy.
C. Study the sexual differences between men and women, described above, and discuss which differences apply to you in your marriage.

Answers to Chapter 8

1. workmanship
2. conception
3. change, defeat
4. physical, mental/emotional, intuitive, sexual
5. taller, heavier, hair
6. skeletal, trunk
7. life expectancy, outlive
8. larger, smaller
9. water
10. muscle
11. work, accomplishments, relationships
12. personal, interest
13. wider, details
14. feelings, emotions, ideas, judgements
15. aloud, options
16. speak, decision, solution
17. compartments, separate
18. holistic, blend, fuse
19. change, adapt
20. observation
21. constant
22. lower
23. preparation, emotional, mental

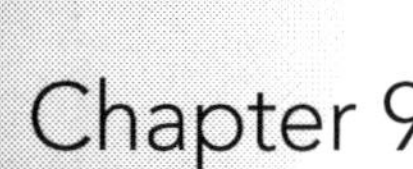

Chapter 9

SEX IS GOOD, SEX IS GODLY

Chapter Overview

- Sex was God's idea and it was designed solely for the environment of marriage.
- Outside of the context of marriage, God considers it a sin, with many deleterious consequences.
- Sex is like money and power. It is neither good, nor bad. Rather, it assumes the character of whoever controls it.
- Having sex regularly can do more than make you feel closer to your partner – it can actually make you physically ______________.

A. Hidden health benefits of sex

1. Feelings of intimacy and relaxation; good sex helps to combat ______________, and stave off anxiety and depression;
2. Another benefit of good sex is sounder ______________;
3. The endorphins that are released during an orgasm closely resemble morphine, and they effectively relieve ______________;
4. Sex helps boost your body's ______________ to illness by up to 30 per cent;
5. It keeps the skin and body looking ______________ and more ______________;
6. Sex enhances ______________, boosts confidence and promotes ______________;

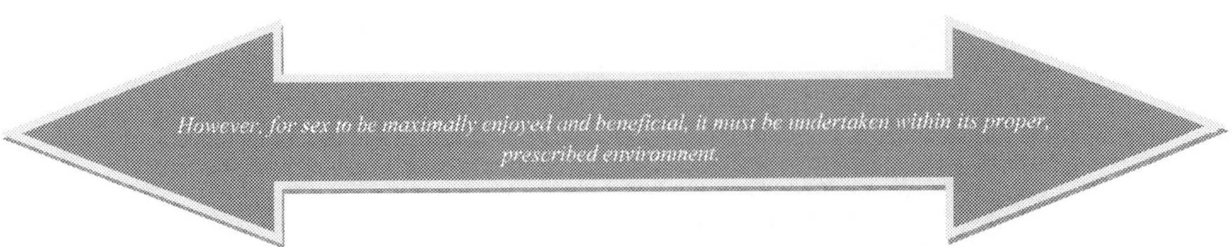

B. What is the proper environment for sex? The one who ______________ man and induced him with his sexuality also determined the 'rules of engagement':

- The first, logical and natural, inference of this statement is that God is both male and female;
- Next God 'blessed them' and instructed them to 'be fruitful and multiply and replenish the earth...'
- Thirdly, they were to literally and figuratively fill and ______________ the earth.

So God created man 'in his own image, in the image of God created he him' (Gen. 1:26–27; Gen. 2:25).

C. Sex was designed by God for the institution of marriage.

D. Three major purposes of sex:

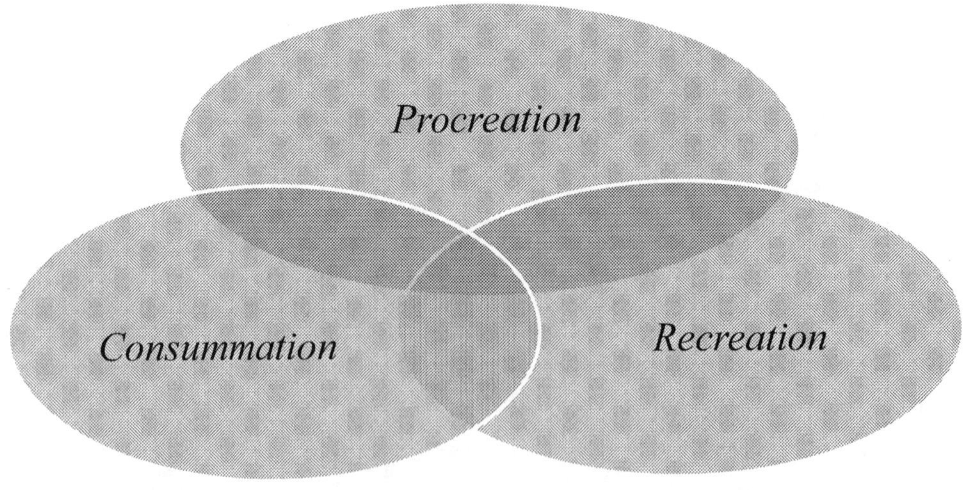

1. Procreation

Sex is thus the primary key to fulfilling the divine mandate of fruitfulness, multiplication, replenishment and dominion.

Didn't God create you to become like one person with your wife? And why did he do this? It was so you would have children, and then lead them to become God's people. Don't ever be unfaithful to your wife. (Malachi 1:15 CEV)

2. Consummation

Sex is given by God as the rite and symbol of the consummation of a ______________ between a man and his wife within a marital union – the most ______________ relationship that can exist between man and wife.

3. Recreation

Sex is also designed by God for ______________, fun and ______________.

E. Sex typifies worship

- every legitimate activity between a married couple reflects an aspect of the Christ–Church ______________;
- When, therefore, a man and his wife come together in sex, what they do embodies the exalted act of ______________.

F. The outer court

- A husband must 'get ______________' with his wife before he attempts to access her 'holy of holies'. He must be ______________ in spirit, soul and body.
- Cleanliness is next to godliness.

G. The holy place – behind the veil

- Before a man can demand or expect sexual relationship with his wife, there must be ______________ and an unhindered flow of communication;

- there must be ______________ in the way a man talks to and about his wife, and in the way he relates with her;
- A husband must ______________ up his wife's life, blow her mind, and always be a revelation;
- The veil also represents the covering that a man must always give his wife if he expects ultimate sexual ______________;
- A husband must shield his wife from his parents, friends and what Job calls 'the scourge of the tongue'.
- He must also physically secure the place where he and his wife are being intimate.

H. The holiest of all

- This represents the place of deepest communion and intimacy between a man and his wife;
- It is the point at which their spirits, souls and bodies fuse;
- It is of necessity preceded by the marital vows and commitment, role definition and implementation, effective and positive communication, and appropriate conflict resolution techniques.

I. The woman's obligations

a) Planning: the woman's primary duty is to provide a loving ______________, and a ______________ that will make his assignment not just fruitful but ecstatic to boot;
b) Prioritise sex: seize the moment, go with the flow, and deal with how you feel. Never underestimate the force of the male sex drive, nor ever forget how critical to a man's ______________ his sexual fulfilment is;
c) Sleep like a log:

    - one of the challenges to a couple's sex life is physical and mental ______________;
    - If, after a nice long rejuvenating nap, you are still making excuses, then you are sending strong ______________ signals to your husband;

d) Where, when and how?

    - Good sex can be had anywhere that is safe, private and decent;

- Utilise all the rooms in your house, and do not be shy to explore new positions;
- There is no standard for how often one should be having sex;
- Each couple must find their rhythm and what works best for them; and even that is variable;
- do not ______________ or defraud your partner too often.

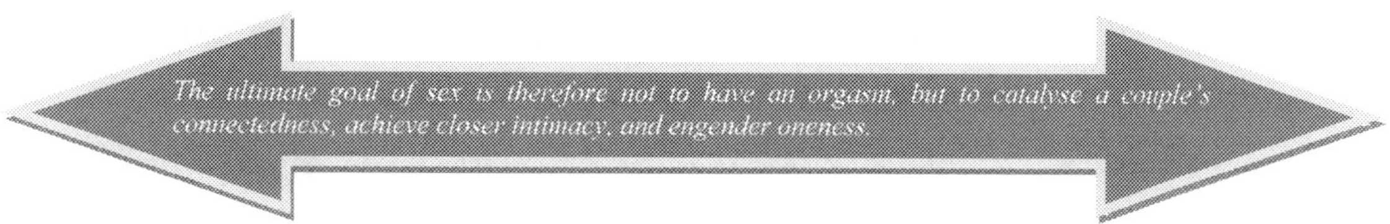

Forbearing one another in love; endeavouring to keep the unity of the Spirit in the bond of peace. (Eph. 4:2–3)

J. Sexual problems are solvable

a) Sexual dysfunction:

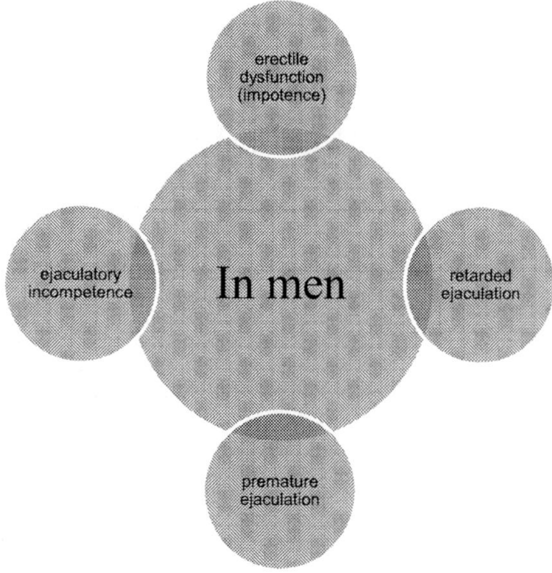

In women

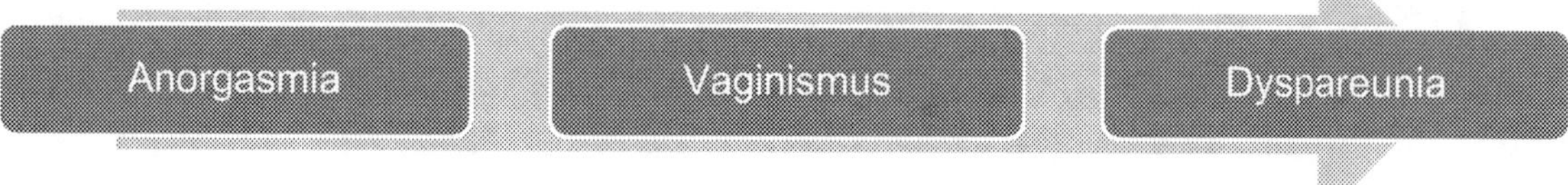

b) Some tips that will help prevent or mitigate the effect of threatened or actual sexual dysfunction:

1. Firstly:

    i. sex is not a ____________, a race, or a job to be done;
    ii. it is an occasion for exploration and intimacy;
    iii. once understood, it removes the pressure to perform or have sex 'the right way', which causes the anxieties that leads to dysfunction.

2. Secondly:

    iv. neither you nor your spouse is clairvoyant;
    v. keep the lines of communication open effectively.

3. Thirdly:

    vi. take everything you read or hear about sex with a pinch of salt.

4. Fourthly:

    vii. if you run into sexual problems of any kind, talk to your spouse about them and walk through the solution together.

K. What is taboo for a Christian couple? What is permissible sexually for a sanctified couple to engage in?

Three particular scriptures can help you lay a framework:

Hebrews 13:4 *says: 'Have respect for marriage. Always be faithful to your partner, because God will punish anyone who is immoral or unfaithful in marriage' (CEU). The authorised version says 'marriage is honourable in all, and the marriage bed undefiled...'*

1COR 7:5 *gives sex advice: 'So don't refuse sex to each other, unless you agree not to have sex for a little while, in order to spend time in prayer. Then Satan won't be able to tempt you because of your lack of self-control.'*

***1 COR 6:12** 'All things are lawful to me, but not all things are profitable [are helpful –ESU]'. 'All things are lawful for me, but I will not be brought under the power of any [but I won't allow anything to gain control over your life – GW]'.*

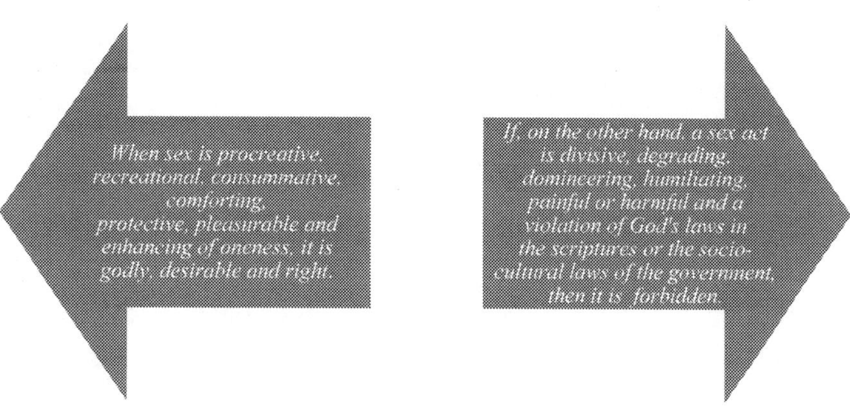

L. Five clear areas are to be avoided by godly couples when engaging in sex:

a) no external parties;

Galatians 5:19, Ephesians 5:3, Colossians 3:5, 1 Thessalonians 4:3

b) no pornography;

1 John 2:16–17

c) no violence;
d) nothing enslaving or illegal;
e) nothing that violates the conscience or sensibility of one or both partners is permitted.

M. Oral sex

- use of the mouth and tongue to stimulate and delight a partner's genitalia;
- Song of Songs speaks of oral sex in a positive and poetic fashion.

In Song of Songs 2:3 it appears the woman has taken the man's 'fruit' in her mouth.

In Song of Songs 4:12–5:1 the husband compares his wife's nude and nubile form to a garden effervescing with fragrant scents and flavours, while comparing her moist vagina to a fresh spring.

- If man and wife are comfortable with the practice, oral sex is biblically permissible but must never be forced on an unwilling partner, nor can it be allowed to substitute for vaginal ____________ union.

D. Masturbation

This is erotic stimulation, especially of one's own genital organs, commonly resulting in orgasm, and achieved by manual or other bodily contact exclusive of sexual intercourse, by instrumental manipulation, occasionally by sexual fantasies, or by various combinations of these agencies.

- the Bible has no problem with manual stimulation, which is a spouse masturbating their partner as a part of ____________;
- it must, however, not take the place of actual coitus.

E. Anal sex

- the Bible strictly ____________ homosexual sex;
- the Bible is, however, silent on the act of anal sex between a heterosexual couple.
- when in doubt, err on the side of the ____________ and/or caution.

F. Menstrual sex

- If both partners are ____________ with the act then it is permissible.

G. Role-playing/sexy lingerie

- role-playing is acting out a mutually agreed fantasy, including dressing up for the part;
- it is not sinful or unhealthy, unless a thought of outsiders, or trying to look like someone specific, comes into the equation;
- it should also be avoided if it becomes an obsession, or central to a couple's love-making routine;

- since men are visual, every wife should build up a wardrobe of sexually stimulating attire.

H. Sex toys

- used in a proper way and with proper items, there is no Biblical injunction against sex toys, as they are a relatively modern invention;
- if they are used as enhancement aids and not a substitution for proper sex, then they are acceptable;
- if one partner is more involved, or excludes the other, or uses the aids by themselves, then it becomes counterproductive or even sinful.

I. Birth control

There are five types of birth control:

Faith

- *This is when a Christian couple trusts God alone to regulate the number of children they will have. This may work for some people, especially if both partners are in complete agreement, but may not work for most.*

Natural Birth Control

- *This is a system whereby pregnancy is avoided by the abstention from coitus on days when the wife is likely to be fertile.*

Non-Abortive Birth Control

- *These are better methods that prevent the sperm and egg from coming together. Examples include: the male condom; the diaphragm; the contraceptive sponge; cervical caps; and female condoms. It also includes temporary female sterilization and male vasectomy, which are permanent forms of birth control.*

Abortive Birth Control.

- *Oral contraceptives, generically known as 'the pill', inhibit ovulation.*
- *They also thicken the cervical mucus, making sperm travel to the egg more difficult.*
- *Thirdly, the pill shrinks the lining of the uterus so that it is impossible or difficult for the facilitation of the implantation of the newly fertilised egg.*

Outright Abortion.

- *Killing a fertilised egg is what abortion is about. Medical procedures, the morning-after pill, the intra-uterine device (IUD) and Norplant are all clear examples of abortive murder which kills off an already conceived child. Pro-life Christians will therefore not have anything to do with these ungodly methods of birth control.*

J. Kissing, necking and petting

- _______________ is kissing and caressing amorously, mainly involving the top parts of the body;
- _______________ is engaging in amorous embracing, caressing and kissing;

- kissing, necking and petting are actual sexual activities, and are a vital part of foreplay for a married couple.

K. Cyber sex

- This is when a couple use modern technology such as 'sexting', phone, email, webcasts or videos to communicate sexually.
- This is permissible if no one else is involved or gains access to recorded or other personal materials, which is virtually impossible in cyberspace.

Conclusion

An admonition to couples with regard to sex is to respect the word of God and their partner's conscience:

- No one is to force, cajole, intimidate or browbeat their partner into doing what they are not comfortable with;
- We are to ____________ the other person to ourselves;
- We must also not violate our ____________ in our search for thrills or so-called sexual liberty.

Remember, the just shall live by faith and whatsoever is not of faith, is sin.

Application Section

SEX

This Application Section consists of two sections: the individual section and the interactive section. Make sure you have enough time to interact with each other during the interactive section

Individual (Spouse) Section

Set the scene: Remain together as a couple, but complete this section on your own.

Goal: To gain knowledge about yourself as a reflection of God.

Directions: Rate your sexual relationship with your spouse. Circle the number that corresponds to your answer. Write down what you think your spouse's answer will be, *with 'A' being the least and 'E' being the most.*

A B C D E	The quality of your sex life
A B C D E	The frequency of your physical intimacy
A B C D E	The variety of your intimacy together
A B C D E	The depth/level of your spiritual intimacy
A B C D E	Satisfaction after intercourse
A B C D E	Quality and level of foreplay
A B C D E	Selflessness during love-making

Write down the answers to the following questions:

1. Do you have any fears about sex?
2. Are you open, giving and loving towards your spouse during sex?
3. During lovemaking and/or foreplay, I would like my spouse to ____________
4. When my spouse and I are making love, I will ____________________________
5. How can you improve you sex life with your spouse?

Interactive (couple) section

Set the scene: Couple to stay together in a private area to talk freely.

Goal: To gain knowledge about each other and your vision and view of the purpose of your marriage.

Directions: Discuss your answers above with your spouse.

Please note: Counselling is available for any couple going through any sexual issue within their marriage.

Homework:

1. Schedule time to read Song of Solomon together.
2. Plan a weekend getaway or a day away, and enjoy a time of intimacy with your spouse.

Answers to Chapter 9

1. healthier
2. stress
3. sleep
4. pain
5. immunity
6. younger, vibrant
7. happiness, relaxation
8. created
9. replenish
10. covenant
11. intimate
12. enjoyment, pleasure
13. relationship
14. worship
15. right, clean
16. friendship
17. sweetness
18. light
19. intimacy
20. environment, response

21. self-acceptance
22. fatigue
23. rejection
24. deprive
25. competition
26. sexual, foreplay
27. forbids, conscience
28. comfortable
29. necking, petting
30. prefer
31. consciences

Chapter 10

FATAL ATTRACTIONS AND DISASTROUS DISTRACTIONS

Chapter Overview

- An attraction means being drawn to a person or thing that appeals to your natural or excited interest, emotion or aesthetic sense.
- Every couple is susceptible to, and has been embraced by, the allure of extramarital attraction.

I. What is extramarital attraction?

a) An extramarital attraction is an ____________, that is, an attraction that arouses hope or desire;
b) At some point in our marital lives, we will meet someone other than our spouses that will cause ____________ in our hearts;
c) Some attractions will be 'close encounters of the fleeting kind' and will therefore not be ____________.

d) Other attractions will be longer-lasting and will develop into torrid ___________.

e) Even the most ardent of temptations is still not sinful: it remains an inducement that must be violently ___________ and put down.

'For we do not have a high priest who is unable to feel sympathy for our weaknesses, but we have one who has been tempted in every way, just as we are – yet he did not sin' (Hebrews 4:15)

II. What to look out for
– Beware of your 'The One' complex:

a) God used your ___________, your ___________ and your ___________ to lead you to choose the right person for you.
b) God may have brought you two together but it will take ___________ ___________ and ___________ on both your parts, to keep you together.
c) God may have provided you the piano and the accompanying hymn sheets, but you have to make your own music and stop a stranger, or usurper, from fiddling with your instruments.

'Wherefore let him that thinketh he standeth take heed lest he fall. There hath no temptation taken you but such as is common to man…' (1 Corinthians 10:12)

III. Watch out for your 'specs':

a) Each of us is attracted to a ___________ ___________ of person.
b) Our specifications ('specs') are a web of looks and other sensory stimuli, personality types, hates and likes, aversions, predictions, desires and revulsions, abusers and enhancers: what attracts you, what 'turns you on'.
c) Often we do not know why we are drawn to a ___________ ___________ of person, but we know we are.
d) Admitting to your spouse what ___________ you in the opposite sex will help you reach a place of ___________ and relative safety.
e) Your spouse can erect a safety net around you when you are around a person/ people who attract you.
f) Your partner will help meet some of your needs where such needs are godly and realistic, and not irrational or ungodly.

IV. No angels in marriage:

a) Marriage is a perfect institution run by two ____________ people.
b) According to Selwyn Hughes, "the greatest single obstacle to a successful Christian marriage is trying to get your spouse to meet your basic ____________ ____________.
c) You have no right to expect ____________ from your spouse, when you cannot provide it.
d) However This is my conclusion., again according to Selwyn Hughes, you can actually find ____________, but only in Christ, when you decide to make Him your personal ____________ and Saviour.

V. Delineate boundaries from the outset:

a) Many contemporary Christians, married and single, see nothing wrong about playful or romantic teasing with members of the opposite sex, also known as ____________.
b) '____________ banter', which makes everyone feel good about themselves, is the erroneous label we give to this dangerous preoccupation.
c) But ____________ can be instantaneous.
d) It is critical that each couple outlines the physical and emotional ____________ that regulate their relationships with those of the opposite sex.

Boundaries will include no intimate contact like hugging, embracing, kissing, calling anyone else by suggestive pet names, no dining alone with external parties, no discussion of private, family or intimate matters, and any others as agreed between each couple.

Remember your marriage is private and 'the heart of deceitful above all things, and desperately wicked: who can know it? (Jeremiah 17:9). So God's word advises us to 'keep thy heart with all diligence for out of it are the issues of life' (Proverbs 4:23, KJV). The BNIV puts it like this: 'Above all else, guard your heart, for it is the wellspring of life.'

VI. Expose to Depose:

a) One of the devil's primary weapons is ____________;

b) The most devastating thing you can do to your marriage is to keep your spouse in the dark about an extramarital attraction;
c) In the dark, secret places of our hearts may lurk the poisonous fruits of a ________________ attraction, such as sexual and erotic fantasies;
d) We cannot afford to let sleeping dogs lie. We must dig out all that causes us to sin;
e) Those thoughts which are ____________ in our subconscious are to be expressed to our partners because if they are repressed, they will cause long-term ____________.
f) We may ____________ ourselves into believing that only if sex is involved is there any harm.
g) However, ____________ could begin in your heart: this rules out taking solace in your secret fantasy world, 'where after all nobody has been harmed and no physical union has taken place' (Proverbs 23:7a KJV).
h) Only a very small number of adulterous dalliances are ____________, ____________ and ____________.

Remember that concealing stuff, even an attraction , from your partner does not protect them, as we may deceive ourselves into believing. Rather, concealment endangers both you and your marriage.

VII. Do not defraud each other:

a) God prefers people to get married rather than to indulge in ____________; see 1Corinthians 7:9.
b) the marital union is the safe house for sexual ____________; the husband must oblige his wife by fulfilling his ____________ duties to her, as she must indeed fulfil hers to him; see 1 Corinthians 7:1-5
c) To withhold sex, companionship, emotional support, comfort and a listening ear from your spouse is therefore to 'defraud' them;
d) According to Merriam-Webster online dictionary, to defraud is to ____________, or deprive someone of something by deception or fraud;
e) Deprivation exposes the deprived person to a greater likelihood of extra-marital ____________ and adultery; this is implied by 1 Corinthians 7:5
f) We have a responsibility to be emotionally and sexually involved with our spouses;

g) Satisfy your spouse, emotionally and sexually, and nothing else will hold enough allure to drag them into indiscretion and sin.

VIII. Six myths and facts about extramarital affairs extracted from research conducted by Dr Shirley Glass:

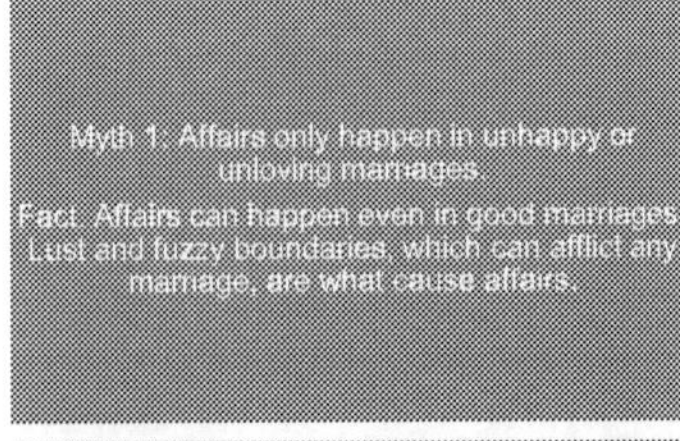

Myth 1: Affairs only happen in unhappy or unloving marriages.

Fact: Affairs can happen even in good marriages. Lust and fuzzy boundaries, which can afflict any marriage, are what cause affairs.

Myth 2: Affairs occur mostly because of sexual attraction.

Fact: Sexual attraction is one of the ingredients. Being the object of adoration, respect and desire of a potential new lover also play an important part. The excitement of novelty, new roles, and the opportunities for growth that a new relationship engenders, also contribute in no small measure to extra-marital affairs

Myth 3: A cheating spouse almost always leaves clues, so a naive spouse must be burying his or her head in the sand.

Fact: This is not necessarily true as the majority of affairs are never detected while they are going on. The Bible and experience, however, show that the secret will ultimately be exposed. Many individuals can compartmentalise their lives so effectively that they can conceal affairs. Others are just such brilliant inveterate liars that they can successfully pull the wool over their partner's eyes.

Myth 4: A person having an affair shows less interest in sex at home.

Fact: This is not usually the case as the enticement of an affair can actually increase passion at home, and make sex even more interesting. This is in part because the perpetrator has convinced him or herself that 'variety is the spice of life'. Also, they could carry the after-glow from their amours to their marriage bed. Before someone says, 'Well, that can only be a good thing!' This is a short-term benefit with devastating long-term consequences.

Myth 5: The person having an affair isn't 'getting enough' at home.

Fact: This is as ridiculous as the suggestion that everyone who steals has a pressing need. Some people's warped rationale is that they are getting all they want and need and so they are looking for something 'dangerous', 'on the edge' or 'outside the box'. One thing is for sure though, the unfaithful partner is not giving enough, and so is less invested than their spouse, who is giving more - or indeed their all.

Myth 6: A straying partner finds fault with everything you do.

Fact: This is not typical. In fact, some become ultra nice to avoid casting the shadow of suspicion on themselves. Usually, they would tend to alternate between being very critical and being very affectionate.

VIII. Three steps to avoid fire:

a) Do not focus on the attraction as that will only encourage and feed it;
b) Turn on the recording device of your conscience and play back to the problem emotion the moral imperatives that are recorded there;
c) Take the steps that are necessary to break off a close association.

IX.'Help! My Bosom's On Fire!' If the extramarital attraction becomes fatal and you actually succumb to adultery, what should you do?

a) First step is to ____________ your sins:

- to yourself;
- to God;
- to your spouse;
- to your pastor, mentor or 'vertical accountability partner'.
- Proverbs 28:13 warns that the one who conceals his sin will not prosper; however, God will be merciful to anyone who confesses their sins and stops doing wrong.

b) Responsibilities for the 'the offender':

- Since trust has been betrayed, a sense of trust has to be restored over a period of time;
- The onus is mostly now on the offender to prove their continuing commitment to a monogamous relationship;
- They must communicate sincere remorse and a strong, believable promise not to relapse.
- At the initial stages at least, they must be willing to answer questions about the affair.
- The offender must accept that most or all of their future endeavours will be strictly monitored and evaluated.

a) The confession:

- Firstly, timing is everything, and the place where it is done is critical;
- Secondly, decide where you want to conduct this sacred trust of an assignment;
- Thirdly, planning ahead is preferable to spontaneity;
- Finally, also, don't rush things. Do not expect instant forgiveness, though by grace you may get just that;

b) Steps for the 'the offended party' to take:

- Find it in your aching, broken heart to ____________ your partner: forgiveness accelerates the healing process, and facilitates rehabilitation and recovery;
- Do not fall into the common trap of believing that your spouse's infidelity was your fault, or that it proves you are not worthy of love;
- Reason together and talk things through with the offender, trying get to the root cause of the affair;
- Go forward: it is impossible to go forward and give space for the rebirth of the relationship when you cannot stop looking backwards;
- Lastly, take a holiday, to help heal your marriage. Not necessarily a trip anywhere, but take a holiday from discussing the issue, once a resolution has been reached.

Conclusion

Adultery can be deadly, strength-sapping, financially ruinous and socially disgraceful. A wise man is therefore to stay with, and be satisfied sexually by, his wife alone (Proverbs 5:15–16 BNIV; Proverbs 5:21–23 BNIV). The best, most sustained and most satisfying sex is to be found in marital relationships.

Application Section

FATAL ATTRACTIONS AND DISASTROUS DISTRACTIONS

This Application Section consists of two sections: the individual section and the interactive section. Make sure you have enough time to interact with each other during the interactive section.

Individual (Spouse) Section

Set the scene: Remain together as a couple, but complete this section on your own.

Goal: To gain knowledge about yourself as a reflection of God.

Directions: Get a pen and paper and write your answers to these questions:

1. Has your marriage gone through the issue of a 'fatal attraction'?
2. List the boundaries you have with regard to attraction to someone other than your spouse?
3. Do you fully trust your spouse? If not, in what area is trust lacking?

Interactive (couple) section

Set the scene: Couple to stay together in a private area to talk freely.

Goal: To gain knowledge about each other, and your vision and view of the purpose of your marriage.

Directions: 1. Share and discuss as a couple the work you completed in the individual section.

Homework:

1. Pray together, schedule a date night and keep this date.
2. Make a commitment to improve communication and intimacy between you and your spouse.

Answers to Chapter 10

1. enticement
2. palpitations
3. problematic
4. temptations
5. resisted
6. feelings, intellect, will
7. hard work, patience
8. certain kind, certain kind
9. attracts
10. accountability
11. imperfect
12. personal needs
13. perfection, perfection
14. Lord
15. flirting
16. Harmless
17. attraction
18. boundaries
19. ignorance
20. fatal
21. suppressed, damage
22. deceive
23. adultery
24. spontaneous, unexpected, unplanned
25. fornication
26. liberty, conjugal
27. cheat
28. attraction
29. confess
30. forgive

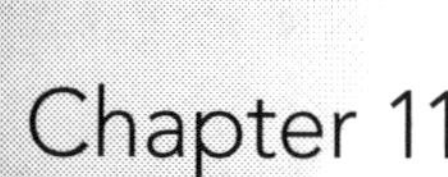

Chapter 11

RAISING GODLY CHILDREN

Chapter Overview

Has not the one God made you? You belong to him in body and spirit. And what does the one God seek? Godly offspring. So be on your guard, and do not be unfaithful to the wife of your youth. (Malachi 2:15)

- Children are God's ingenious device for the perpetuation of the human species.
- 'A baby is God's opinion that the world should go on' (Carl Sandburg).
- Marriage is, however, the only divinely prescribed environment for the bringing forth and raising of godly children.

A. Parents are to learn to successfully raise their children in spite of the problems that oppose their efforts (Proverbs 22:6).
B. If God is the archetypal father, then wisdom dictates that anyone willing to raise godly children must of necessity learn from him.
C. Twelve characteristics of God as a father which earthly parents must emulate in their God-given task of raising Godly seed:

1. A father ____________ and ____________.

   - To beget is to ____________ as the father, or to sire;

- Godly parents should therefore ____________ the spirits, souls and bodies of children;
- Children are to be taught that they are ____________ who have a duty of worship to their Creator in spirit and in truth;
- Children must be taught that their bodies are the ____________ of God's Holy Spirit, who dwells in them.

2. A father ____________ and ____________.

   - Parents are to prop up their children so they can stand up on their own.

3. The father ________________

   - Parents are expected to protect their children from ____________ external influences.

4. A father ____________ and disciplines.

   - Discipline provides ____________ for the lawless and disobedient, for the ungodly and the sinners (1Tim 1:9 KJV; Proverbs 13:24 BNIVUK).

5. Four major forms of discipline:

Rebuke or chasten with words	Spanking (Proverbs 23:13-14 KJV)	Withdrawal of privileges	Increased responsibility and the law of consequences

6. A father ____________ and appreciates:

   - Love is so vital because it represents the very ____________ of God; see 1 John 4:7-8;
   - Love is abstract, God defines and exemplifies it through practical applications;
   - God's love resulted in His gift of His son. Your love will be substantiated by your giving the ____________ to your children that is within your power;
   - Children are God's ____________ and reward, (Psalm 127:3) and if parents do not appreciate them, they will depreciate them instead.

7. A father __________ (John 1:12)

    - Parents have to __________ their children, in line with God's purpose for their lives.
    - Seven 'principles of purpose' as outlined by Dr Myles Munroe:

        a) God is a God of purpose;
        b) everything in life has a purpose;
        c) not every purpose is known;
        d) wherever purpose is not known, abuse is inevitable;
        e) if you want to know the purpose of a thing, never ask the thing;
        f) purpose is only found in the mind of the creator;
        g) purpose is the key to fulfilment.

8. A father leads, directs and exemplifies (Romans 8:14):

    - Children learn more from what they see their parents do than what their parents try to teach them (Proverbs 22:6);
    - According to Brigham Young, we should never permit ourselves to __________ anything that we are not willing to see our children __________.

9. A father leaves an __________:

    - *A good man leaveth an __________ to his children's children. (Proverbs 13:22)*

10. A father __________ a name:

    - A good name is rather to be chosen than great riches, and loving favour rather than silver and gold; (Proverbs 22:1)
    - A disgraceful name sets a child back in ways that are multitudinous and complex.

'Solomon loved the lord, walking in the statutes of David his father' (1 Kings 3:3 KJV). Solomon was thus to enjoy the 'sure mercies of David'. In 2 Samuel 7:12–15 God even promised that if he sinned, he would be chastened with floggings inflicted by men, but God's love would never be taken away from him, as it was from Saul.

11. A father loves his wife – the child's mother – ___________ and ___________.

A true father would:

- love his wife, the mother of his children, for better or for worse.
- will teach his children likewise to love their own spouses, and also
- teach them to patiently go through the fire and the flood, and coming out on the other side in a safe and prosperous place.

3. A father builds his child's sense of ___________:

- by cultivating in them a sense of uniqueness and developing their individual talents, so that they will make an impact on their world;
- he teaches them early on that they are 'in the world, but not of it';
- he chooses their friends for them;
- he teaches them to avoid close alliances with children from athreistic, immoral, carnal, rebellious or worldly families;
- he creates the time to cultivate their child's innate ability so that when the right opportunities arise for them to impact their world, they can grab them with both hands.

4. A father cultivates his child's sense of self-worth:

- confidence and satisfaction in oneself;
- a sense of self-respect;
- knowing you are a person of ___________ in the eyes of the world around you.
- The responsibility for cultivating your child's sense of self-worth lies squarely with you, the parents.

- *As Christian parents, you also need mentors.*
- *You must identify more mature Christian couples who have successfully trodden where you are headed.*
- *They must have utilised divine principles to raise God-fearing, obedient and respectful children.*

Finally, raising children is a joint responsibility of both parents. It is not done accidentally or by trial-and-error, must be discussed and pre-planned before marriage, must be constantly reviewed and consistent. Parents must have a plan of action so that problems don't arise with raising their children. Raising godly seed is not by any person's might or power, but by God's grace and the work of His Spirit in our lives.

Having done all to stand, we should pray always with all prayers and supplication in the Spirit. (Ephesians 6:18)

Application Section

RAISING GODLY CHILDREN

This Application Section consists of two sections: the individual section and the interactive section. Make sure you have enough time to interact with each other during the interactive section.

Individual (Spouse) Section

Set the scene: Remain together as a couple, but complete this section on your own.

Goal: To gain knowledge about yourself as a reflection of God.

Directions: Get a pen and paper and write your answers to these next questions.

Write down the different ways you are empowering and raising your children.

Interactive (couple) section

Set the scene: Couple to stay together in a private area to talk freely.

Goal: To gain knowledge about each other, and your vision and view of the purpose of your raising your children.

Directions: 1. Discuss your list together.

2. Write one point of action you will both take, individually and as a couple, towards raising your children.

Homework:

1. Schedule time to discuss specific character qualities we want to see cultivated in the life of your children.
2. Discuss how you both can work together to instil spiritual training for your children. Put a plan together, and ensure it is executed correctly.

Answers to Chapter 11

1. begets, creates
2. procreate
3. nourish
4. spirit-beings
5. temple
6. nurtures, strengthens
7. protects
8. harmful
9. chastens
10. boundaries
11. loves
12. nature
13. best
14. heritage
15. empowers
16. empower
17. do, do
18. inheritance
19. inheritance
20. bequeaths
21. unconditionally, eternally
22. significance
23. value

Chapter 12

TILL DEATH DO US PART

Chapter Overview

- o Couples must carefully consider the above aspect of their marital ____________.
- o This is because marriage can be likened to ____________ ____________, with your spouse as your ____________ ____________.
- o Marriage is not to be entered into ____________, unadvisedly and ____________. The Word of God stipulates that marriage is for life.
- o Society ____________ from strong, healthy marriages.
- o The primary purpose of marriage is to illustrate the wonderful and unique relationship between Christ and the Church.
- o A broken home leads to broken spouses, broken children and a broken society.

God has designed marriage to withstand every eventuality. His word assures us that 'No temptation has overtaken you except what is common to mankind. And God is faithful: He will not let you be tempted beyond what you can bear. But when you are tempted, He will also provide a way out so that you can endure it' (1 Corinthians 10:13).

I. Prominent Bible characters have faced and ____________ some of the thorniest issues that could bedevil and rock even the most stable of Christian homes:

   a) Adam and Eve lost paradise but did not lose one another; they witnessed one son exiled because he had murdered his brother;
   b) Abraham and Sarah were another remarkable couple who dealt with issues such as:

      - decades of ____________;
      - Sarah's disingenuous scheme with Hagar, her maid;

- the covetous attraction to Sarah of two powerful kings;
- and the issue of a mistress and her illegitimate child.

c) Isaac and Rebecca waited for ____________ years before they had children. They also faced fierce ____________ challenges (see Genesis 26).
d) Elizabeth and Zacharias continued to faithfully serve God even into their old age when it appeared that all hope and likelihood of having a child was long lost.

II. Secrets of a lifelong marriage?

a) The first and most vital key is to start your marital relationship (as indeed any other relationship or endeavour) with a ____________ from God;
b) The second key is to use ____________ principles to solve every marital problem.

III. It's all about love:
The foundation of every marriage and relationship is love, because God is love. There are four different Greek words translated as *love* in English:

EROS
- Greek word from which we get the word *erotic*. It is physical, passionate love with sensual desire and longing.
- It is a need-oriented love that yearns for sensual expression.

PHILEO
- Affectionate regard or friendship;
- Companionship, not just desire;
- Secrets are shared here.

STORGE
- This kind of love is centred around affection.
- It is the kind of natural affection associated with kinship.
- It is the kind of love felt by parents for their offspring, and siblings for one another.

AGAPE
- The true unconditional love of God (1 John 4:7-8), as contrasted with the attraction suggested by *eros*, the friendship built over time and on account of shared interests as implied by *phileo*, and the natural affection on account of being related as suggested by *storge*.

IV. Qualities of agape love:

- It is ____________: it therefore gives and expects nothing in return;
- It is ____________ and ____________: spontaneous and unmotivated;
- It is impervious to human ideas of ____________: there was no contribution, worthiness, work or value on our part in the process of salvation (Romans 5:8);
- It bequeaths value on those who are ____________.

Can you now see how if these four qualities of agape are applied to a long-deceased, moribund relationship, they can work wonders? Many marriages start to fail when spouses become selfish, self-centred, egotistical and arrogant or when people get tired, frustrated or

Conclusion

You made a vow to one another that only death could part you. If you decide and intend to keep that vow, God will give you the grace and resources to do just that.

Application Section

TILL DEATH DO US PART

This Application Section consists of two sections: the individual section and the interactive section. Make sure you have enough time to interact with each other during the interactive section.

Individual (Spouse) Section

Set the scene: Remain together as a couple, but complete this section on your own.

Goal: To gain knowledge about yourself as a reflection of God.

Directions: Get a pen and paper and write your answers to these next questions.

Instructions: Rate the different types of love, and describe how these have affected and/or are still affecting your relationship.

Types of love	What effect does this have on your relationship?	Effects on your marriage caused by this love, or lack.
•Eros	• Little ☐ • Some ☐ • Significant ☐	• Little ☐ • Some ☐ • Significant ☐
•Phileo	• Little ☐ • Some ☐ • Significant ☐	• Little ☐ • Some ☐ • Significant ☐
•Storge	• Little ☐ • Some ☐ • Significant ☐	• Little ☐ • Some ☐ • Significant ☐
•Agape	• Little ☐ • Some ☐ • Significant ☐	• Little ☐ • Some ☐ • Significant ☐

Interactive (couple) section

Set the scene: Couple to stay together in a private area to talk freely.

Goal: To gain knowledge about each other, and your vision and view of the purpose of your marriage.

Directions: 1. Discuss between yourselves your answers to the above individual section.

2. Write down one point of action you will take, individually or as a couple, to show *agape* love.

Homework:

1. Write a love letter to your spouse and exchange this letter before the next class.
2. Scriptures to meditate on at home with your spouse: John 1:1; Genesis 2:24; Genesis 12:2–3.

Answers to Chapter 12

1. vows
2. life imprisonment, cell mate
3. blindly, precipitously
4. benefits
5. overcome
6. infertility
7. twenty, financial
8. word
9. divine

IV. Qualities of *agape* love:

1. selfless
2. instinctive, unforced
3. value
4. undeserving

Printed in the United States
By Bookmasters